SCIENTIFIC AMERICAN™
Critical Anthologies on Environment and Climate™

CRITICAL PERSPECTIVES ON
THE OCEANS

Edited by Krista West

The Rosen Publishing Group, Inc., New York

Published in 2007 by The Rosen Publishing Group, Inc.
29 East 21st Street, New York, NY 10010

First Edition

The articles in this book first appeared in the pages of *Scientific American*, as follows: "Diversity Blues" by Marguerite Holloway, August 1994; "Counting the Last Fish" by Daniel Pauly and Reg Watson, July 2003; "Shrimp Aquaculture and the Environment" by Claude E. Boyd and Jason W. Clay, June 1998; "Red Tides" by Donald M. Anderson, August 1994; "Alarming Nets" by David Schneider, September 1996; "The Rising Seas" by David Schneider, March 1997; "The Man Who Would Hear Ocean Temperatures" by Philip Yam, January 1995; "Melting Away" by Sarah Simpson, January 2000; "The Ocean's Invisible Forest" by Paul G. Falkowski, August 2002; "Down and Out in the Gulf of Mexico" by David Schneider, April 1995; "Sounding Out Science" by Marguerite Holloway, October 1996; "Fishy Business" by Sarah Simpson, July 2001; and in the pages of *Scientific American Special Edition*, as follows: "The Origins of Water on Earth" by James F. Kasting, *New Light on the Solar System*, 2003; and in the pages of *Scientific American Presents*, as follows: "Life in the Ocean" by James W. Nybakken and Steven K. Webster, *The Oceans*, Fall 1998.

Library of Congress Cataloging-in-Publication Data

Critical perspectives on the oceans/edited by Krista West.—1st ed.
    p. cm.—(Scientific American critical anthologies on environment and climate)
Includes bibliographical references and index.
ISBN 1-4042-0692-2 (library binding)
1. Oceans—Juvenile literature. 2. Marine ecology—Juvenile literature. I. West, Krista. II. Title. III. Series.
GC21.5.C75 2007
551.46—dc22

2005031182

On the cover: Soft coral with fish using the reef to protect them, off Komodo Island, Indonesia.

CONTENTS

Introduction

"Knowledge of the oceans is more than a matter of curiosity," President John F. Kennedy told Congress in 1961. "Our very survival may hinge upon it." Nearly half a century later, these words still ring true. Scientists now understand that the oceans play two major roles on Earth. As a life supporter, most of the life on the planet lives in the oceans. As a climate regulator, the oceans move and store heat. Between these two roles, the oceans deserve a lot of credit for making Earth what it is today.

A History of Exploration

Ocean exploration by the United States officially began in 1807, when President Thomas Jefferson created a government agency called the United States Coast Survey to study the country's coastlines. These early scientists concentrated on mapping the edge of the sea and the character of the seafloor. They took the temperature of the world's oceans, determined the direction of water currents, and cataloged life-forms. Over the next hundred years, the development of new technologies governed much of our ability to explore the oceans. Getting to many places in the ocean isn't easy, so scientists had to invent ways to get to these remote places. Dredges (large scoops used to scrape the deep sea for life) and early forms of sonar were among the inventions that helped scientists study ocean life and layout.

Today, nearly two centuries later, the original United States Coast Survey has become part of the National Oceanic and Atmospheric Administration (NOAA), which conducts research on the oceans, atmosphere, space, and the sun. Modern researchers continue to build upon the knowledge of the early ocean explorers by studying sea life and the seafloor. This knowledge helps us get to know the oceans better. Once we know and understand the oceans, we can better monitor overall ocean health.

The Role of the Oceans

Scientific exploration of the oceans in the past two centuries has uncovered many mysteries of the sea, including the sheer size of the oceans on Earth. We now know 71 percent of the planet is covered with ocean—and that's just surface area. To really get a sense of the size of the oceans, it helps to consider the volume of the planet's biosphere. The biosphere is all parts of Earth that can support life. It includes places on land, in the air, and in the oceans. Imagine that the volume of Earth's biosphere is contained in a super-size, thirty-two-ounce soda cup. Of the biosphere in this cup, almost thirty ounces are ocean. Given the immense size of the oceans, it's not surprising that they hold a lot of life. Of the thirty-three animal phyla (or categories of animals) on Earth, thirty consist of ocean residents.

Once you have some idea of the size of the oceans and their importance as a home for life on Earth, consider the role the oceans play in Earth's weather. When asked what controls the weather on our planet, you might naturally look to the sky. However, the sky works with the oceans as an equal partner to make our weather. Together, the sky and the oceans have been called the planet's thermostat.

The planet gets plenty of heat from the sun, but because of the way Earth spins, most of that heat settles in the equatorial regions in the middle of the globe. The oceans work together with the winds to move the heat around Earth. Without this movement of heat, the middle of the planet would fry and the poles would be completely (instead of partially) frozen.

The Future of the Oceans

Ocean science seems to be at a pivotal point in time. We have a good enough understanding of ocean basics that we are beginning to examine

ocean health. Over time, changes in the oceans—
perhaps caused by humans—could have an
impact on the rest of the planet.

The idea of changes happening in the oceans
is a fairly new one. At one time, the oceans
were seen as so large and limitless it seemed
impossible that human activity could have any
impact. Only recently have scientists had the
knowledge or resources to measure any changes.
Not surprisingly, this is where the controversial
stuff comes in. Changes in the oceans are still
difficult to measure, and even harder to make
sense of. But more and more scientists are
sounding alarms that the oceans are changing,
perhaps for the worse. So many alarms are going
off that the politicians and government officials
that make ocean laws are starting to listen.

The area of the ocean the United States
controls is bigger than the area of land that makes
up the country. Despite this fact, there are far
fewer policies and rules to govern ocean use and
protection than there are to govern the land.
Making matters worse, many experts believe the
policies that do exist to govern the oceans are
outdated.

In 2004, a report recommending changes
was published that should help the United States
update its policies. The sixteen-member
Commission on Ocean Policy, a federal group of
ocean experts in charge of developing a policy

plan for the oceans, put out the report, entitled "An Ocean Blueprint for the 21st Century." The report contains dozens of very specific recommendations targeted to specific federal agencies to change how the oceans are managed. For example, recommendation 20-8 states, "The National Oceanic and Atmospheric Administration and U.S. Department of the Interior agencies should develop an expanded program, coordinated through the National Ocean Council, to examine and mitigate the effects of human activities on marine mammals and endangered species."

The level of detail and direction makes the recommendations pretty clear, but reading through the report can make you a little dizzy because there is so much that the experts say needs to be done. In general, the recommendations include suggestions to do the following:

- Enhance government leadership to protect the oceans
- Coordinate ocean management regionally
- Fund more ocean education
- Control coastal water and vessel pollution
- Create a network of scientists to monitor the oceans
- Prevent the spread of invasive species
- Make fishing sustainable
- Make aquaculture sustainable
- Support more ocean research

- Manage ocean energy resources, including deep-sea drilling for natural gas
- Create an ocean observing system

If you're interested in learning more about the oceans and why they need to be protected, this book is a great place to start. The following articles were written by or about experts in ocean science and first published in *Scientific American* magazine. The first chapter will fill you in on ocean basics, the following two chapters deal with changes in ocean life and temperature that scientists are watching closely, and the last chapter looks at specific places in the oceans where interesting things are happening. As you read, keep in mind that this is just a small sampling of what scientists have learned about the oceans so far. Humans have studied the oceans for centuries (at least), and our interest doesn't seem to be dwindling. —*KW*

1 Earth's Oceans

The oceans hold water that is essential to life on Earth. But why are the oceans here? Scientists studying the planet have a good idea why the land formed (plate tectonics), and an even better idea of the age of the planet (about 4.6 billion years). But Earth didn't start off with water—and no other planets are known to have water—so why does Earth have water and where did it come from?

The leading theory suggests early Earth was like a giant bucket catching incoming balls of ice from outer space. Scientists hypothesize that the ice balls were most likely frozen meteorites and comets. Eventually, Earth collected enough ice balls to create the oceans and an atmosphere developed that helped keep the water on the planet.

Still up for debate is where in space these meteorites and comets came from. Some suggest they came from the asteroid belt between Mars and Jupiter, others say they came from beyond Jupiter. By studying the type of hydrogen found in ocean water and comparing it to the hydrogen

*found in certain comets, scientists are beginning
to solve the mystery. —KW*

"The Origins of Water on Earth"
by James F. Kasting
*Scientific American Special Edition: New Light on
the Solar System*, 2003

Of all the planets, why is Earth the only one fit for
life? Simple: because Earth has a surface that supports
liquid water, the magic elixir required by all living
things. Some scientists speculate that forms of life
that do not require water might exist elsewhere in the
universe. But I would guess not. The long molecular
chains and complex branching structures of carbon
make this element the ideal chemical backbone for life,
and water is the ideal solvent in which carbon-based
chemistry can proceed.

Given this special connection between water and
life, many investigators have lately focused their
attention on one of Jupiter's moons, Europa.
Astronomers believe this small world may possess an
ocean of liquid water underneath its globe-encircling
crust of ice. NASA researchers are making plans to
measure the thickness of ice on Europa using radar
and, eventually, to drill through that layer should it
prove thin enough.

The environment of Europa differs dramatically
from conditions on Earth, so there is no reason to
suppose that life must have evolved there. But the

very existence of water on Europa provides sufficient motivation for sending a spacecraft to search for extraterrestrial organisms. Even if that probing finds nothing alive, the effort may help answer a question closer to home: Where did water on Earth come from?

Water from Heaven

Creation of the modern oceans required two obvious ingredients: water and a container in which to hold it. The ocean basins owe their origins, as well as their present configuration, to plate tectonics. This heat-driven convection churns the mantle of Earth—the region between the crust and core—and results in the separation of two kinds of material near the surface. Lighter, less dense granitic rock makes up the continents, which float like sponges in the bath over denser, heavier basalt, which forms the ocean basins.

Scientists cannot determine with certainty exactly when these depressions filled or from where the water came, because there is no geologic record of the formative years of Earth. Dating of meteorites shows that the solar system is about 4.6 billion years old, and Earth appears to be approximately the same age. The oldest sedimentary rocks—those that formed by processes requiring liquid water—are only about 3.9 billion years old. But there are crystals of zirconium silicate, called zircons, that formed 4.4 billion years ago and whose oxygen isotopic composition indicates that liquid water was present then. So water has been on Earth's surface throughout most of its history.

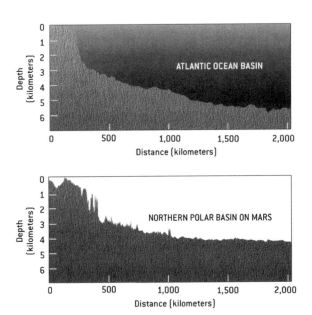

Topographic mapping of Mars has recently revealed remarkable similarities to the ocean basins on Earth. For example, the western Atlantic near Rio de Janeiro (*top*) presents a similar profile to that of the northern polar basin on Mars (*bottom*).

Kevin J. Zahnle, an astronomer at the NASA Ames Research Center, suggests that the primordial Earth was like a bucket. In his view, water was added not with a ladle but with a firehose. He proposes that icy clumps of material collided with Earth during the initial formation of the planet, injecting huge quantities of water into the atmosphere in the form of steam.

Much of this water streamed skyward through holes in the atmosphere blasted open by these icy planetesimals themselves. Many of the water molecules

(H_2O) were split apart by ultraviolet radiation from the sun. But enough of the initial steam in the atmosphere survived and condensed to form sizable oceans when the planet eventually cooled.

No one knows how much water rained down on the planet at the time. But suppose the bombarding planetesimals resembled the most abundant type of meteorite (called ordinary chondrite), which contains about 0.1 percent water by weight. An Earth composed entirely of this kind of rubble would therefore have started with 0.1 percent water—at least four times the amount now held in the oceans. So three quarters of this water has since disappeared. Perhaps half an ocean of the moisture became trapped within minerals of the mantle. Water may also have taken up residence in Earth's dense iron core, which contains some relatively light elements, including, most probably, hydrogen.

The initial influx of meteoric material probably endowed Earth with more than enough water for the oceans. Indeed, that bombardment lasted a long time: from 4.5 billion to 3.8 billion years ago, a time called, naturally enough, the heavy bombardment period.

Where these hefty bodies came from is still a mystery. They may have originated in the asteroid belt, which is located between the orbits of Mars and Jupiter. The rocky masses in the outer parts of the belt may hold up to 20 percent water. Alternatively, if the late-arriving bodies came from beyond the orbit of Jupiter, they would have resembled another water-bearing candidate—comets.

Comets are often described as dirty cosmic snow-balls: half ice, half dust. Christopher F. Chyba, a planetary scientist at the University of Arizona, estimates that if only 25 percent of the bodies that hit Earth during the heavy bombardment period were comets, they could have accounted for all the water in the modern oceans. This theory is attractive because it could explain the extended period of heavy bombardment: bodies originating in the Uranus-Neptune region would have taken longer to be swept up by planets, so the volley of impacts on Earth would have stretched over hundreds of millions of years.

Alternatively, the impactors may have come from the asteroid belt region between 2.0 astronomical units (AU, the mean distance from Earth to the sun) and 3.5 AU. Alessandro Morbidelli of the Observatory of the Côte d'Azur in France and his co-workers have shown that asteroids whose orbits were highly inclined to the plane of the solar system could have continued to pelt Earth for a similar period.

This widely accepted theory of an ancient cometary firehose has recently hit a major snag. Astronomers have found that three comets—Halley, Hyakutake and Hale-Bopp—have a high percentage of deuterium, a form of hydrogen that contains a neutron as well as a proton in its nucleus. Compared with normal hydrogen, deuterium is twice as abundant in these comets as it is in seawater. One can imagine that the oceans might now hold proportionately more deuterium than the cometary ices from which they formed, because normal hydrogen, being lighter, might escape the tug of gravity more easily and be lost to space. But it is difficult to see how the oceans could contain proportionately less deuterium. If these three comets are representative of those that struck here in the past, then most of the water on Earth must have come from elsewhere.

A controversial idea based on observations from satellites suggests that about 20 small (house-size) comets bombard Earth every minute. This rate, which is fast enough to fill the entire ocean over the lifetime of Earth, implies that the ocean is still growing. This much debated theory, championed by Louis A. Frank of the University of Iowa, raises many unanswered questions, among them: Why do the objects not show up on radar? Why do they break up at high altitude? And the deuterium paradox remains, unless these "cometesimals" contain less deuterium than their larger cousins.

More recently, Morbidelli has argued convincingly that most of Earth's water came from the asteroid belt. The ordinary chondrites are thought to come from the inner part of this region (2.0 to 2.5 AU). But outer-belt asteroids (2.5 to 3.5 AU) are thought to be water-rich. According to Morbidelli, as Earth formed it collided with one or more large planetesimals from the outer belt. Gravitational perturbations caused by Jupiter elongated the planetesimal's orbit, allowing it to pass within Earth's orbit. Earth may have picked up additional water from asteroids on highly inclined orbits

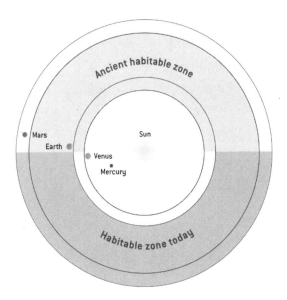

Habitable zone, where liquid water can exist on the surface of a planet, now ranges from just inside the orbit of Earth to beyond the orbit of Mars (*dark gray*). This zone has migrated slowly outward from its position when the planets first formed (*light gray*), about 4.6 billion years ago, because the sun has gradually brightened over time. In another billion years, when Earth no longer resides within this expanding zone, the water in the oceans will evaporate, leaving the world as dry and lifeless as Venus is today.

that arrived during the heavy bombardment period. In this scheme, no more than 10 percent of Earth's water came from comets that originated farther out in the solar system. This theory is consistent with deuterium-hydrogen ratios, which indicate that the comets' watery contributions were small.

The Habitable Zone

Whatever the source, plenty of water fell to Earth early in its life. But simply adding water to an evolving planet does not ensure the development of a persistent ocean. Venus was probably also wet when it formed, but its surface is completely parched today. How that drying came about is easy to understand: sunshine on Venus must have once been intense enough to create a warm, moist lower atmosphere and to support an appreciable amount of water in the upper atmosphere as well. As a result, water on the surface of Venus evaporated and traveled high into the sky, where ultraviolet light broke the molecules of H_2O apart and allowed hydrogen to escape into space. Thus, this key component of water on Venus took a one-way route: up and out.

This sunshine-induced exodus implies that there is a critical inner boundary to the habitable zone around the sun, which lies beyond the orbit of Venus. Conversely, if a planet does not receive enough sunlight, its oceans may freeze by a process called runaway glaciation. Suppose Earth somehow slipped slightly farther from the sun. As the solar rays faded, the climate would get colder and the polar ice caps would expand. Because snow and ice reflect more sunlight back to space, the climate would become colder still. This vicious cycle could explain in part why Mars, which occupies the next orbit out from Earth, is frozen today.

The actual story of Mars is probably more complicated. Pictures taken from the Mariner and Viking probes and from the Global Surveyor spacecraft show that older parts of the Martian surface are laced with channels carved by liquid water. Measurements from the laser altimeter on board the Global Surveyor indicate that the vast northern plains of Mars are exceptionally flat. The only correspondingly smooth surfaces on Earth lie on the seafloor, far from the midocean ridges. Thus, many scientists are now even more confident that Mars once had an ocean. Mars, it would seem, orbits within a potentially habitable zone around the sun. But somehow, eons ago, it plunged into its current chilly state.

A Once Faint Sun

Understanding that dramatic change on Mars may help explain nagging questions about the ancient oceans of Earth. Theories of solar evolution predict that when the sun first became stable, it was 30 percent dimmer than it is now. The smaller solar output would have caused the oceans to be completely frozen before about two billion years ago. But the geologic record tells a different tale: liquid water and life were both present as early as 3.8 billion years ago. The disparity between this prediction and fossil evidence has been termed the faint young sun paradox.

The paradox disappears only when one recognizes that the composition of the atmosphere has changed considerably over time. The early atmosphere probably contained much more carbon dioxide than at present and perhaps more methane. Both these gases enhance the greenhouse effect because they absorb infrared radiation; their presence could have kept the early Earth warm, despite less heat coming from the sun. The greenhouse phenomenon also helps to keep Earth's climate in a dynamic equilibrium through a process called the carbonate-silicate cycle. Volcanoes continually belch carbon dioxide into the atmosphere. But silicate minerals on the continents absorb much of this gas as they erode from crustal rocks and wash out to sea. The carbon dioxide then sinks to the bottom of the ocean in the form of solid calcium carbonate. Over millions of years, plate tectonics drives this carbonate down into the upper mantle, where it reacts chemically and is spewed out as carbon dioxide again through volcanoes.

If Earth had ever suffered a global glaciation, silicate rocks, for the most part, would have stopped eroding. But volcanic carbon dioxide would have continued to accumulate in the atmosphere until the greenhouse effect became large enough to melt the ice. And eventually the warmed oceans would have released enough moisture to bring on heavy rains and to speed erosion, in the process pulling carbon dioxide out of the atmosphere and out of minerals. Thus, Earth has a built-in thermostat that automatically maintains its surface temperature within the range of liquid water.

Paul Hoffman and Daniel Schrag of Harvard University have argued that Earth did freeze over at least twice during the Late Precambrian era, 600 to 750 million years ago. Earth recovered with a buildup of volcanic carbon dioxide. This theory remains controversial because scientists do not fully understand how the biota would have survived, but I am convinced it happened. There is no other good way to explain the evidence for continental-scale, low-latitude glaciation. Six hundred million years ago, Australia straddled the equator, and it was glaciated from one end to the other.

The same mechanism may have operated on Mars. Although the planet is now volcanically inactive, it once had many eruptions and could have maintained a vigorous carbonate-silicate cycle. If Mars has sufficient stores of carbon—one question that NASA scientists hope to answer with the Global Surveyor—it could also have had a dense shroud of carbon dioxide at one time. Clouds of carbon dioxide ice, which scatter infrared radiation, and perhaps a small amount of methane would have generated enough greenhouse heating to maintain liquid water on the surface.

Mars is freeze-dried today not because it is too far from the sun but because it is a small planet and therefore cooled off comparatively quickly. It was unable to sustain the volcanism necessary to maintain balmy temperatures. Over the eons, the water ice that remained probably mixed with dust and is now trapped in the uppermost few kilometers of the Martian crust.

The conditions on Earth that formed and maintain the oceans—an orbit in the habitable zone, plate tectonics creating ocean basins, volcanism driving a carbonate-silicate cycle, and a stratified atmosphere that prevents loss of water or hydrogen—are unique among the planets in our solar system. But other planets are known to orbit other stars, and the odds are good that similar conditions may prevail, creating other brilliantly blue worlds, with oceans much like ours.

The Author

James F. Kasting received his bachelor's degree in chemistry and physics from Harvard University. He went on to graduate studies in physics and atmospheric science at the University of Michigan at Ann Arbor, where he obtained a doctorate in 1979. Kasting worked at the National Center for Atmospheric Research and for the NASA Ames Research Center before joining Pennsylvania State University, where he now teaches in the departments of geosciences and meteorology. Kasting's research focuses on the evolution of habitable planets around the sun and other stars.

Earth's oceans hold more life than its land. But ocean life is complicated and often foreign to us land lovers. In the ocean, life-forms are surrounded by water, not air. Some places have sunlight, some don't. Some places are warm and some are really cold. Some places are shallow, some deep.

These different ocean environments provide a home for a variety of life-forms. Of great *interest to modern ocean scientists is the life in the deepest parts of the ocean where heat is scattered and light is nonexistent. Here, scientists are learning that there are many different species of life, but not many members of any one species. The authors of the following article suggest that these small populations are most likely due to the unreliability of food trickling down from surface waters and the extreme pressures found at these depths.*

Or perhaps we just haven't found all the lifeforms yet. Scientists estimate 90 percent of the oceans remain unexplored, which means there may be entire populations and types of life that remain undiscovered and not yet described. There is still much to do and learn. —KW

"Life in the Ocean"
by James W. Nybakken and Steven K. Webster
Scientific American Presents: The Oceans, **1998**

Earth is misnamed. Even though the planet is largely made up of rock, 71 percent of its surface is covered with ocean. Like the wet film coating a newly washed plum, this water makes up a thin layer compared with the globe as a whole. Yet that watery veneer comprises more than 90 percent of the biosphere by volume: it covers 360 million square kilometers (140 million square miles) and runs, on average, a few kilometers deep. It is in these salty depths that life first emerged four billion years ago, and it is there that life continues to teem today in many strange forms. This blue planet would be better dubbed Oceanus.

The ocean has long been mysterious, its interior largely inaccessible. And although it may not hold the sea monsters that mariners once envisioned, it continues to hold many questions for scientists. Researchers have studied less than 10 percent of the ocean and, because of the difficulty of getting safely to the bottom, have explored no more than 1 percent of the deep ocean floor. Marine biologists know most about the near-shore environments—the coasts, the coral reefs, the kelp forests—and a few other areas that divers can study with ease. But researchers remain ignorant about many aspects of oceanic ecosystems, particularly about life in the midwaters—those between the light-filled upper 100 meters (328 feet) and the near-bottom realm of the deep sea.

From what investigators do know, it is clear that marine animals display a greater diversity of body types than land animals do. Their scientific description requires more broad categories—that is, more phyla (the second most general taxonomic grouping)—than are needed to categorize their terrestrial cousins. Of the 33 animal phyla, 30 describe residents of the ocean, 15 exclusively so. Only 16 phyla include animals found on land or in freshwater—and of those, only one is exclusively terrestrial. This phenomenon reflects the fact that life evolved in the sea and that few life-forms were able to adapt to the absence of water around their bodies.

Yet at the species level, the reverse appears to be true. One and a half million terrestrial species have been described—mostly insects and vascular plants—but total estimates range from five million to more than 50 million. Of the organisms that live in the ocean, however, only 250,000 species have been identified; total estimates run closer to 400,000 to 450,000. This count may change considerably once scientists get a better grasp of life on the ocean floor: some experts posit that between one million and 10 million benthic species have yet to be described.

Watery Properties

From people's often terrestrially biased perspective, marine organisms can seem odd. Some of these creatures glow in the dark, many are soft and boneless, and most saltwater plants grow fast and die young—unlike trees, which live to a ripe old age. These differences have arisen because of the physical and chemical characteristics of the ocean.

Seawater is about 800 times as dense as air and is much more viscous. Therefore, marine organisms and particles of food can float endlessly through the water—whereas no creatures drift permanently in the air. Because small life-forms and organic particles are constantly wafting about, some sea animals spend their lives fixed in place, grazing on food in the water around them; on land, only spiders achieve anything like this sedentary lifestyle. The density of water also buoys up organisms, obviating the need for structural supports of cellulose or bone to counteract gravity.

Life underwater has a unique hue as well. Water absorbs light differently than air does. Shorter wavelengths—such as those of the blues and greens—penetrate more deeply than the longer wavelengths of the reds and yellows do. So the view 10 meters below the surface is mostly blue. A few hundred meters deeper there is no sunlight at all and hence no photosynthesis. The midwater and deep-sea communities must depend on the photosynthesizers that reside in the sunlight-filled surface waters. As they sink, these microscopic phytoplankton, zooplankton and decaying particles sustain the fauna of the deep sea.

This rain of plant food is hardly constant, however. Phytoplankton are seasonal and vary by region. Most of the larger species—the ones that turn the ocean green or brown or red when they bloom—thrive in coastal and certain equatorial areas where nutrients are abundant. Much smaller species—called prochlorophytes—are found in tropical and mid-ocean waters. Bottom-dwelling large algae, such as kelp, and seed plants, such as surf grasses, are confined to such a restricted shallow zone around the continents and islands that they contribute little to the overall biological productivity of the ocean, which is relatively modest.

The ocean does not contain much plant life, because concentrations of critical nutrients are lower than they are on land. Phosphorus and nitrogen, for example, are present at only 1/10,000 of their concentration in

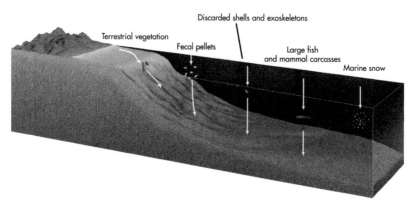

Terrestrial vegetation

Discarded shells and exoskeletons

Fecal pellets

Large fish
and mammal carcasses

Marine snow

The creatures of the ocean are extremely diverse, reflecting the varied conditions in which they live. Many marine organisms stay in the upper waters, feeding on the zooplankton and phytoplankton found there. For their part, residents of the ocean bottom exist in darkness and under great pressure. Most of the scant food supply in this realm originates in the shallows (*diagram above*). For now, at least, the lowest depth that scientists can safely visit is about 6,500 meters (21,300 feet), and so their knowledge of the creatures of the deep seafloor is limited.

fertile soil. As a consequence, the ocean supports only a small fraction of what can be grown on reasonably productive land. One cubic meter of soil may yield 50 kilograms (110 pounds) of dry organic matter a year, but the richest cubic meter of seawater will yield a mere five grams of organic matter in that same interval.

The global distribution of what few nutrients there are depends largely on the temperature stratification of the ocean. In the tropics, surface waters are always quite balmy; in temperate regions, these upper waters

warm in the summer and are cold the rest of the year.
Below the well-mixed surface layer is a narrow zone—
called the thermocline—that separates the warm
surface from the colder, and thus heavier, water beneath.
(An exception to this common configuration occurs
near the poles, where the upper and lower levels of the
ocean are equally cold.)

It is this cold, heavy water that is the key to the
food chain. Because it receives a constant rain of
organic detritus from above, deep, chilly water is
richly supplied with nutrients. And because no light
reaches it, no photosynthesis takes place there—so few
organisms take advantage of this abundant nourish-
ment. In contrast, surface water is often barren of
nutrients because the sun-loving photosynthesizers
have depleted them.

In the tropics, the separation between the
warmth at the surface and the cold at depth is so
great that even hurricanes and typhoons cannot
completely mix the two. As a result, the waters of
the tropics remain bereft of nutrients and of the
phytoplankton that depend on them. Lacking these
clouds of microscopic life, tropical seas normally stay
crystal-clear. In temperate regions, winter storms can
churn up the ocean, bringing some of the nutrients
to the surface. In certain places such as coasts, where
steady winds blow the warm surface waters offshore,
deep waters rise to take their place. Such areas of
nutrient-rich water support some of the world's
largest fisheries.

Under Pressure

Temperature and depth also play an important role because these variables control the availability of oxygen. On land, air provides plants and animals with a fairly constant mixture of this life-giving gas: 210 milliliters per liter. In the sea, oxygen enters only at or near the surface. And because most of the water found in the deep ocean originated at the surface in the coldest parts of the world, it sank carrying large amounts of dissolved oxygen. These water masses may spend centuries in the deep sea before they rise again to the surface. But because life is sparse and moves slowly down there, oxygen is rarely depleted. So, strangely, the ocean is often most oxygen depleted at intermediate depths. For example, in certain areas of the Pacific Ocean an "oxygen minimum zone" occurs between 500 and 1,000 meters below the surface. Only a few organisms are adapted to life in this oxygen-poor environment. Most creatures just travel through it quickly on their way to the surface or back down, where the water is richer in oxygen.

Life in that deep realm is under a great burden. Every 10 meters of seawater adds roughly another atmosphere of pressure: at one-kilometer depth the pressure is 100 atmospheres (100 times what people normally experience). In the profoundest ocean trenches, the pressure reaches more than 1,100 atmospheres. Many invertebrates and some fishes can tolerate the trip from one kilometer deep up to the surface—if they do not have gas-filled sacs that expand as they ascend—and can then survive at one atmosphere for years in refrigerated aquariums.

Despite this opportunity to study them in tanks, marine biologists know relatively little about the organisms that live down in those cold, dark regions. Investigators have learned only that the inhabitants of these realms have unusual adaptations that equip them to live in this environment. For this reason, they are some of the most interesting of all oceanic residents.

The Deepest Mystery

Recent studies of the deep sea suggest that although the diversity of species is high, their density is quite low. Food for these organisms arrives in the unending shower of organic particles called marine snow—although sometimes a large carcass, a clump of kelp or a waterlogged tree may settle on the seafloor. Of these sources, though, the marine snow is the most important. As it sinks toward the bottom, microbes, invertebrates and fishes feed on it—and so there is less and less to fall downward. This diminishing supply means there are fewer and fewer consumers at greater depth.

Even more important than the meager, uneven supply of food are the effects of pressure. Deep-sea animals and invertebrates with shells tend to be gelatinous and to have sluggish movements. Their shells are poorly developed because it is difficult to accumulate calcium carbonate under high pressure. If the creatures have skeletons, they are lightweight. Most deep-sea animals are also small. Many midwater fishes, for instance, are no more than 20 centimeters long. But there are exceptions. Giant squid may reach 20 meters. And the largest comb jellies and siphonophores (relatives of the Portuguese man-of-war) live in the midwater zone, where the absence of strong currents and waves enables these delicate animals to achieve astounding proportions. In fact, the longest animal in the world appears to be a siphonophore of the genus *Praya*, which grows to 40 meters in length and is only as thick as a human thumb. Comb jellies can become the size of basketballs, and the mucus house of the giant tadpole-shaped larvacean *Bathocordaeus charon* may be as large as a Great Dane.

Many of these ghostly creatures glow in their dark abode [see "Light in the Ocean's Midwaters," by Bruce H. Robison; SCIENTIFIC AMERICAN, July 1995]. Bioluminescence can be found in 90 percent of the midwater species of fish and invertebrates, and many deep-sea fishes have relatively large eyes, so they can see by this faint light. The luminosity serves a variety of purposes: to identify and recognize species, to lure potential prey, to startle a predator and to warn mates of dangers. At depths of a few hundred meters, where dim light still penetrates, the light enables some organisms to blend in with the brighter surface and render their silhouettes invisible from below. Other advantages probably exist that scientists have not yet discovered.

Although they are able to flash light, midwater fishes are often black in color, and many of the crustaceans are red. Because red light cannot penetrate into deep water, this color provides excellent camouflage. Some large jellyfish and comb jellies tend to be purple or red as well.

The top carnivores, which roam near the surface, seldom have such tints. Tuna, billfish, whales, dolphins, seals, sea lions and even seabirds often move through well-lit surroundings as they travel sometimes thousands of kilometers every year. Their movements to feed— whether they are going from deep water to the surface or moving around the globe—result in the longest migrations of animals on the planet.

Some of these creatures have come to represent sea life for most people, so it remains amazing how little biologists know about their habits. How do sperm whales dive a kilometer deep to locate and capture giant squid? Do the yellowfin tuna of the tropical and the semitropical Pacific intermingle? Or are they separate genetic stocks? Part of the reason for this paucity of knowledge is that whales and open-water fishes are extremely difficult to study because they roam the world. Some whales, for example, migrate every year to feed in areas of cold upwelling near the poles and then travel again to reproduce in warmer latitudes. These creatures are the living oil tankers of the sea: using their blubber as fuel, they undergo vast fluctuations in weight, sometimes losing 30 percent of their body mass during migration.

Right Under Our Feet

Not surprisingly, the ocean communities and creatures that researchers know best are those nearest shore: coral reefs, sea-grass beds, kelp forests, coastal mangroves, salt marshes, mudflats and estuaries. These areas are the places people fish, dive, dig for clams, observe shorebirds and, when not paying attention, run boats aground. As a result, these habitats are also the ones people have damaged most severely.

Such environments constitute less than 1 percent of the ocean floor by area, but because they are shallow, well lit and adjacent to landmasses, concentrations of nutrients and biological productivity are relatively high. These coastal areas also link saltwater and freshwater environments. Anadromous fishes, such as salmon, striped bass, shad and sturgeon, reproduce in freshwater rivers and streams, but their offspring may spend years feeding in the ocean before they return to complete the cycle. Catadromous fishes, such as the American and European eels, do the opposite, spending most of their lives in freshwater but going to sea to reproduce.

Perhaps the most familiar near-shore communities of all are those of the intertidal zone, which occupies a meter or two between the high- and low-tide marks. This intertidal stratum is inhabited almost exclusively by marine organisms—although deer, sheep, raccoons, coyotes and bears visit occasionally, as do some insects and a wealth of shorebirds. Organisms living there must be able to endure dryness, bright sunlight and severe shifts in temperature during low tide, as well as the mechanical wear and tear of the waves—which can produce forces equivalent to typhoon winds. It is not surprising, then, to find hard-shelled animals that grip rocks or hide in crevices living there: limpets, periwinkles, barnacles and mussels. Intertidal plants and animals usually occupy distinct horizontal bands that become more densely populated and rich in species at the deeper—and therefore more protected—extreme.

The composition of these littoral communities varies with the shoreline. Sandy shores, for instance, are constantly churned by the waves, so no plants or animals can get a grip for long. Instead most inhabitants are found burrowing underneath the surface. Some tiny animals—called meiofauna—actually live in the interstitial spaces between grains of sand.

Weather patterns and seasonal variations also influence the makeup of the intertidal zone. Temperate areas have the most developed intertidal communities because summer fogs often protect creatures from direct sunlight. In contrast, rocky shores in the tropics are usually quite bare—consisting of a few diatoms, coralline red algae, cyanobacteria, chitons and nerites (both of which are mollusks).

Farther offshore sit the "rain forests" of the marine world: kelp beds and coral reefs. These ecosystems are mutually exclusive but similar in some ways. Both require abundant sunlight and grow within 30 meters or so of the surface. Both contain dominant species that provide a massive, three-dimensional foundation for the community—giant kelp and reef-building corals, respectively. And both house a vast number of species, although coral reefs surpass kelp forests in this regard.

Despite these similarities, their differences are also dramatic. Coral reefs are almost exclusively confined to the tropics, where sea-surface temperatures do not fall below 18 degrees Celsius (about 64 degrees Fahrenheit). Kelp forests do poorly in waters this warm; they are best adapted to temperatures between six and 15 degrees C.

Kelp forests are dominated by the large, brown algae for which they are named. The giant kelp (*Macrocystis pyrifera*) can reach 60 meters in length, stretching 30 meters from the seafloor to the surface and then floating to create a thick canopy. Kelp grow very quickly—as much as half a meter a day in some places. Ninety percent of this plant matter is eaten immediately or washes away to the beach or deep sea, where herbivores later consume it.

These aquatic trees soften the waves and currents and provide food and shelter for many kinds of fish and invertebrates. They are principally grazed by sea urchins and abalone, marine invertebrates that are delicacies for humans and sea otters alike. In some years the urchins get the upper hand, eating the local kelp and other algae—and some invertebrates—to near extinction. It may take several years before the giant kelp can reestablish itself. But in areas where sea otters abound, the urchins are usually kept in check. Indeed, before humans began to hunt for sea otters in the 18th and 19th centuries, populations of urchins and abalones probably never reached the sizes that have supported contemporary commercial fisheries.

Human actions have also profoundly affected many coral ecosystems. These communities are built by stony scleractinian corals, by gorgonians (sea whips and sea fans) and, in the Caribbean, by the hydrozoan fire corals. Scleractinian corals are found in all oceans at a variety of depths. But only the tropical, colonial species construct shallow reefs. These species have photosynthetic dinoflagellates (called zooxanthellae) in their gastric tissues—indeed, 80 percent of corals' soft parts can be made of these creatures. The zooxanthellae photosynthesize and provide the corals with food. These symbiotic dinoflagellates also trigger the corals' rapid calcification, which in turn provides the foundation of the reef structure.

Most reef corals need clear water and a depth of no more than 30 meters so that sunlight can reach their zooxanthellae. The reefs usually do not support many fleshy algae, because grazers—such as sea urchins, parrot fish, surgeonfish and damselfish—constantly nibble at any plant growth. In the early 1980s the importance of these grazers was demonstrated when a pathogen killed 99 percent of the long-spined sea urchins in the Caribbean and algae grew unimpeded, crowding out the corals.

A World Ignored

Despite their obvious richness, marine ecosystems have been left out of most discussions about saving biodiversity. Part of the reason is that they are out of sight and, hence, out of mind to many scientists and laypersons alike. Nevertheless, it is important to expand their scope as quickly as possible. Current research suggests that at least 70 percent of the world's fisheries are operating at or beyond sustainable levels, and as human populations grow this pressure will only increase.

The intricate connections between the coastal areas, the surface waters, the midwaters and the deep sea are becoming clearer. If society wants the ocean and its myriad creatures to thrive, people must further study these links—and learn to recognize how human actions can alter, perhaps irrevocably, life in the sea.

The Authors

James W. Nybakken and Steven K. Webster share a long-standing love of marine biology and the ocean. Nybakken is professor of biological sciences at Moss Landing Marine Laboratories, where he teaches marine ecology and invertebrate zoology. He received his Ph.D. in zoology at the University of Wisconsin and is the author of several books on marine ecology. Webster is senior marine biologist at the Monterey Bay Aquarium, which he founded 20 years ago with three colleagues. He received his Ph.D. in biological sciences from Stanford University and has taught coral reef biology for 30 years.

The oceans are biologically diverse. This means they are home to many different forms of plant and animal life. Measuring this level of diversity and how it is changing with time is a hot topic among ocean scientists.

The following article was published after an ocean diversity meeting of the National Research Council, a nonprofit institution that provides policy advice to the United States government. The meeting resulted in a report that said, "The diversity of marine life is being affected dramatically. Effective solutions will require an expanded understanding of the patterns and processes that control the diversity of life in the sea." In other words, we have to understand what is in the oceans before we can hope to protect it.

Most scientists worldwide agree ocean life is in trouble. The United Nations declared 1998 the "International Year of the Oceans" to raise awareness of ocean issues. Unfortunately, it's unclear if much has changed since the following article was published. The question remains: how sick will the oceans get before the world acts? —KW

"Diversity Blues"
by Marguerite Holloway
Scientific American, August 1994

The evidence is everywhere. Populations of fish and
shellfish, of corals and mollusks, of lowly ocean worms,
are plummeting. Toxic tides, coastal development and
pollutant runoff are increasing in frequency and
dimension as the human population expands. The
oceans—near shore and in the abyssal deep—may be
reaching a state of ecological crisis, but, for the public,
what is out of sight is out of mind. "The oceans are in
a lot more trouble than is commonly appreciated," rues
Jane Lubchenco of Oregon State University. "There is
great urgency."

To remedy this situation, marine scientists recently
gathered in Irvine, Calif., to devise a national research
strategy to protect and explore marine biodiversity.
Although the variety of organisms found in the
oceans is thought to rival or exceed that of terrestrial
ecosystems, there is no large-scale conservation effort
designed to protect these creatures. Indeed, there is no
large-scale effort even to understand the diversity
found in saltwater regions.

The National Research Council meeting attendees
first set about establishing their ignorance: the system
they study remains, in large part, a mystery. Several
years ago, for instance, J. Frederick Grassle of Rutgers
University reported that previous estimates of the
number of organisms thriving on the deep-sea floor

were probably too low. In analyzing sediment from an area off the coasts of Delaware and New Jersey, Grassle found 707 species of polychaetes, or worms, and 426 species of crustaceans. All these creatures were harvested in samples taken from boxes that measured only 30 centimeters per side and 10 centimeters in depth. Earlier studies had suggested a total of a mere 273 species of polychaetes.

As researchers at the meeting emphasized repeatedly, even the diversity of areas that have been exhaustively studied is not fully appreciated. New findings about star coral, or *Montastraea annularis*, offer a dramatic example. This organism "is sort of a lab rat of corals," explains Nancy Knowlton of the Smithsonian Tropical Research Institute in Panama. "It is an extremely intensively studied coral." Knowlton and her colleagues have discovered that this single species of coral is, in fact, three species in shallow waters. (There may be even more species in the star corals that inhabit deeper water.) These various species have also been found to be adapted to different depths.

Knowing that diversity is out there, however, has not yet allowed marine researchers to make a stab at species numbers—something their peers on land have been able to do to galvanize public action. "We are not close to making an estimate," Knowlton acknowledges. "Even a seat-of-the-pants guess might be off by an order of magnitude."

Identifying threats to the oceans was less tricky. Although the usual suspects were in the lineup—

including oil spills, the destruction of estuaries, toxic dumping and the introduction of non-indigenous species that outcompete the locals—conference attendees deemed fishing the greatest danger to marine biodiversity. "I was pretty surprised. The impacts of fishing have been at the top of my list for years," says Les Watling of the Darling Marine Center at the University of Maine. "But I thought there was not such a big awareness of that. The biggest problems are usually seen as pollutants or eutrophication." (Eutrophication is caused by excess nutrients from such chemicals as fertilizers and can lead to algal blooms.)

Nevertheless, reports about the global decline of fisheries keep coming in. As Carl Safina of the National Audubon Society outlined in a recent article in *Issues in Science and Technology*, catches of groupers and snappers fell by 80 percent during the 1980s, and the population of swordfish in the Atlantic Ocean has fallen by 50 percent since the 1970s.

In addition to the depletion of fish—which may have far-reaching but little understood ecological effects—fishing often wipes out habitat. By trawling on the seafloor, vessels disrupt bottom communities or coral reefs. Watling cites the destruction of sponges in the Gulf of Maine as one example. Last seen in 1987 on a videotape taken from a submarine, "the sponges are gone. They have been ground off the rocks," Watling states. These sponges may be important nursery habitats for species such as cod—of course, that possibility reveals another marine unknown. "The real problem is that we do not know anything about the first year of life in cod," Watling warns.

A crisis in taxonomy also worried the scientists. Every researcher had a complaint about years going by before he or she could get someone to identify an alga, about seminal papers misidentifying creatures, about graduate students receiving no training in taxonomy. Without good taxonomy, trying to identify and protect diversity becomes moot.

Beyond the challenge of identifying species correctly is the challenge of understanding their interactions. If marine biology is going to help policymakers, it has to be at least somewhat predictive. Even if the effects of climatic change on a certain species are understood, for example, the implications for the entire ecosystem may be obscure. Unpublished studies by Lubchenco about increases in water temperature caused by a power plant in Diablo Cove, Calif., illustrate just this problem. "You could not have predicted the changes that occurred based on a knowledge of the individual species' sensitivity to water temperature," Lubchenco explains. "What is going on is greater than the individual response."

Getting the scientific community to voice concern about the threat to oceanic ecology was the first step, according to conference chairs Cheryl Ann Butman of the Woods Hole Oceanographic Institution and James T. Carlton of Williams College and Mystic Seaport. Designing a research program that will address the issue and receive funding from Congress is the next task at hand.

The most difficult hurdle may be catalyzing public awareness before the marine environment is altered beyond the point of no return. As Butman and Carlton describe, hunting whales may already have altered the oceans irrevocably. Because deep-sea organisms rely on food falling from the surface, large carcasses of whales may have been one of the major sources of nutrients for the bottom of the food chain. The sulfur-rich bones of whales may have provided stepping-stones for sulfur bacteria and other organisms as they moved from hydrothermal vent to vent. Fewer sinking cetaceans may have had important impacts on deep-sea processes.

"Unfortunately, the question is virtually impossible to answer now," Butman comments. "But it certainly would be irresponsible of us to put ourselves in a position like this again—that is, a position where we embark on a dramatic alteration of species diversity, which is what the whaling industry represents—without evaluating the ecological consequences."

2 Changes in Ocean Life

Changes in ocean life can be measured in declining fish populations. To see that, the following article suggests you only have to look at the menu at your local seafood restaurant.

The authors contend humans are "fishing down" the food chain. A food chain shows where each living thing gets its food. Food chains usually start with large animals and work their way to tiny plants. In the ocean, large fish eat small fish, and small fish eat tiny fish, and tiny fish eat microscopic plants and animals.

Humans are often considered the top of the oceanic food chain. We eat large fish like tuna, shark, and salmon. This article by two fisheries researchers argues that because large fish have become harder for fishermen to catch (they've already caught many of them), we have developed a taste for smaller fish further down on the food chain. If we eat all the small fish, we might keep "fishing down" the food chain until there are no more fish left to eat. —KW

"Counting the Last Fish"
by Daniel Pauly and Reg Watson
Scientific American, July 2003

Georges Bank—the patch of relatively shallow ocean just off the coast of Nova Scotia, Canada—used to teem with fish. Writings from the 17th century record that boats were often surrounded by huge schools of cod, salmon, striped bass and sturgeon. Today it is a very different story. Trawlers trailing dredges the size of football fields have literally scraped the bottom clean, harvesting an entire ecosystem—including supporting substrates such as sponges—along with the catch of the day. Farther up the water column, longlines and drift nets are snagging the last sharks, swordfish and tuna. The hauls of these commercially desirable species are dwindling, and the sizes of individual fish being taken are getting smaller; a large number are even captured before they have time to mature. The phenomenon is not restricted to the North Atlantic but is occurring across the globe.

Many people are under the mistaken impression that pollution is responsible for declines in marine species. Others may find it hard to believe that a shortage of desirable food fish even exists, because they still notice piles of Chilean sea bass and tuna fillets in their local fish markets. Why is commercial fishing seen as having little if any effect on the species that are being fished? We suspect that this perception persists from another age, when fishing was a matter of

An Example of "Fishing Down"

Food webs contain fewer steps, or trophic levels, when overfishing occurs. After fishers have taken the largest members of a slow-growing predatory species—such as saithe—they must turn to smaller individuals that have not yet achieved full size. Unlike older saithe, these younger fish are not large enough to catch cod, which normally consume whiting, which in turn usually eat krill-grazing haddock. Instead the small saithe must eat even smaller fish, such as herring, which feed directly on krill. Wiping out larger saithe therefore shortens the food web to four levels instead of six, disrupting ecosystems. Note that actual trophic levels rarely reach six because large fish eat a variety of other fish.

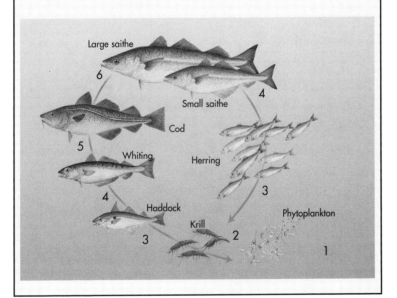

wresting sustenance from a hostile sea using tiny boats and simple gear.

Our recent studies demonstrate that we can no longer think of the sea as a bounteous provider whose mysterious depths contain an inexhaustible resource. Over the past several years we have gathered and analyzed data on the world's fisheries, compiling the first comprehensive look at the state of the marine food resource. We have found that some countries,

Overview/*Fish Declines*

- New analyses show that fisheries worldwide are in danger of collapsing from overfishing, yet many people still view the ocean as a limitless resource whose bounty humanity has just begun to tap.
- Overfishing results from booms in human populations, increases in the demand for fish as a nutritious food, improvements in commercial fishing technology, and global and national policies that fail to encourage the sustainable management of fisheries.
- Solutions to the problem include banning fishing gear such as dredges that damage ecosystems; establishing marine reserves to allow fisheries to recover; and abolishing government subsidies that keep too many boats on the seas chasing too few fish.

particularly China, have overreported their catches, obscuring a downward trend in fish caught worldwide. In general, fishers must work farther offshore and at greater depths in an effort to keep up with the catches of yesteryear and to try to meet the burgeoning demand for fish. We contend that overfishing and the fishing of these distant stocks are unsustainable practices and are causing the depletion of important species. But it is not too late to implement policies to protect the world's fisheries for future generations.

The Law of the Sea

Explaining how the sea got into its current state requires relating a bit of history. The ocean used to be a free-for-all, with fleets flying the flags of various countries competing for fish thousands of miles from home. In 1982 the United Nations adopted the Convention on the Law of the Sea, which allows countries bordering the ocean to claim exclusive economic zones reaching 200 nautical miles into open waters. These areas include the highly productive continental shelves of roughly 200 meters in depth where most fish live out their lives.

The convention ended decades—and, in some instances, even centuries—of fighting over coastal fishing grounds, but it placed the responsibility for managing marine fisheries squarely on maritime countries. Unfortunately, we cannot point to any example of a nation that has stepped up to its duties in this regard.

The U.S. and Canadian governments have subsidized the growth of domestic fishing fleets to supplant those of now excluded foreign countries. Canada, for instance, built new offshore fleets to replace those of foreign nations pushed out by the convention, effectively substituting foreign boats with even larger fleets of more modern vessels that fish year-round on the same stocks that the domestic, inshore fleet was already targeting. In an effort to ensure that there is no opportunity for foreign fleets to fish the excess allotment—as provided for in the convention—these nations have also begun to fish more extensively than they would have otherwise. And some states, such as those in West Africa, have been pressured by others to accept agreements that allow foreign fleets to fish their waters, as sanctioned by the convention. The end result has been more fishing than ever, because foreign fleets have no incentive to preserve local marine resources long-term—and, in fact, are subsidized by their own countries to garner as much fish as they can.

The expansion made possible by the Convention on the Law of the Sea and technological improvements in commercial fishing gear (such as acoustic fish finders) temporarily boosted fish catches. But by the late 1980s the upward trend began to reverse, despite overreporting by China, which, in order to meet politically driven "productivity increases," was stating that it was taking nearly twice the amount of fish that it actually was.

In 2001 we presented a statistical model that allowed us to examine where catches differed significantly from those taken from similarly productive waters at the same depths and latitudes elsewhere in the world. The figures from Chinese waters—about 1 percent of the world's oceans—were much higher than predicted, accounting for more than 40 percent of the deviations from the statistical model. When we readjusted the worldwide fisheries data for China's misrepresentations, we concluded that world fish landings have been declining slowly since the late 1980s, by about 700,000 metric tons a year. China's overreporting skewed global fisheries statistics so significantly because of the country's large size and the degree of its overreporting. Other nations also submit inaccurate fisheries statistics—with a few overreporting their catches and most underreporting them—but those numbers tend to cancel one another out.

Nations gather statistics on fish landings in a variety of ways, including surveys, censuses and logbooks. In some countries, such as China, these data are forwarded to regional offices and on up through the government hierarchy until they arrive at the national offices. At each step, officials may manipulate the statistics to meet mandatory production targets. Other countries have systems for cross-checking the fish landings against import/export data and information on local consumption.

The most persuasive evidence, in our opinion, that fishing is wreaking havoc on marine ecosystems is the phenomenon that one of us (Pauly) has dubbed "fishing down the food web." This describes what occurs when fishers deplete large predator fish at the top of the food chain, such as tuna and swordfish, until they become rare, and then begin to target smaller species that would usually be eaten by the large fish [*see illustration on page 47*].

Fishing Down

The position a particular animal occupies in the strata of a food web is determined by its size, the anatomy of its mouthparts and its feeding preferences. The various layers of the food web, called trophic levels, are ranked according to how many steps they are removed from the primary producers at the base of the web, which generally consists of phytoplanktonic algae. These microscopic organisms are assigned a trophic level (TL) of 1.

Phytoplankton are grazed mostly by small zooplankton—mainly tiny crustaceans of between 0.5 and two millimeters in size, both of which thus have a TL of 2. (This size hierarchy stands in stark contrast to terrestrial food chains, in which herbivores are often very large; consider moose or elephants, for instance.) TL 3 consists of small fishes between 20 and 50 centimeters in length, such as sardines, herring and anchovies. These small pelagic fishes live in open waters and usually consume a variable mix of phyto-plankton and both herbivorous and carnivorous zooplankton. They are caught in enormous quantities by fisheries: 41 million metric tons were landed in 2000, a number that corresponds to 49 percent of the reported global marine fish catch. Most are either destined for human consumption, such as canned sardines, or reduced to fish meal and oil to serve as feed for chickens, pigs and farmed salmon or other carnivorous fish. The typical table fish—the cod, snapper, tuna and halibut that restaurants serve whole or as steaks or fillets—are predators of the small pelagics and other small fishes and invertebrates; they tend to have a TL of between 3.5 and 4.5. (Their TLs are not whole numbers because they can consume prey on several trophic levels.)

The increased popularity in the U.S. of such fish as nutritious foods has undoubtedly contributed to the decline in their stocks. We suggest that the health and sustainability of fisheries can be assessed by monitoring the trends of average TLs. When those numbers begin to drop, it indicates that fishers are relying on ever smaller fish and that stocks of the larger predatory fish are beginning to collapse.

In 1998 we presented the first evidence that "fishing down" was already occurring in some fishing grounds, particularly in the North Atlantic, off the Patagonian coast of South America and nearby Antarctica, in the Arabian Sea, and around parts of Africa and Australia. These areas experienced TL declines of 1 or greater between 1950 and 2000, according to our calculations. Off the west coast of Newfoundland, for instance, the average TL went from a maximum of 3.65 in 1957 to 2.6 in 2000. Average sizes of fish landed in those regions dropped by one meter during that period.

Our conclusions are based on an analysis of the global database of marine fish landings that is created and maintained by the U.N. Food and Agriculture Organization, which is in turn derived from data provided by member countries. Because this data set has problems—such as overreporting and the lumping of various species into a category called "mixed"—we had to incorporate information on the global distribution of fishes from FishBase, the online encyclopedia of fishes pioneered by Pauly, as well as information on the fishing patterns and access rights of countries reporting catches.

Research by some other groups—notably those led by Jeremy B. C. Jackson of the Scripps Institution of Oceanography in San Diego and Ransom A. Myers of Dalhousie University in Halifax—suggests that our results, dire as they might seem, in fact underestimate the seriousness of the effects that marine fisheries have on their underlying resources. Jackson and his colleagues have shown that massive declines in populations of marine mammals, turtles and large fishes occurred along all coastlines where people lived long before the post-World War II period we examined. The extent of these depletions was not recognized until recently because biologists did not consult historians or collaborate with archaeologists, who study evidence of fish consumption in middens (ancient trash dumps).

Myers and his co-workers used data from a wide range of fisheries throughout the world to demonstrate that industrial fleets generally take only a few decades to reduce the biomass of a previously unfished stock by a factor of 10. Because it often takes much longer for a regulatory regime to be established to manage a marine resource, the sustainability levels set are most likely to be based on numbers that already reflect population declines. Myers's group documents this process particularly well for the Japanese longline fishery, which in 1952 burst out of the small area around Japan—to which it was confined until the end of the Korean War—and expanded across the Pacific and into the Atlantic and Indian oceans. The expansion decimated tuna populations worldwide. Indeed, Myers and his colleague Boris Worm recently reported that the world's oceans have lost 90 percent of large predatory fish.

Changing the Future

What can be done? Many believe that fish farming will relieve the pressure on stocks, but it can do so only if the farmed organisms do not consume fish meal. (Mussels, clams and tilapia, an herbivorous fish, can be farmed without fish meal.) When fish are fed fish meal, as in the case of salmon and various carnivores, farming makes the problem worse, turning small pelagics—including fish that are otherwise perfectly fit for human consumption, such as herring, sardines, anchovies and mackerels—into animal fodder. In fact, salmon farms consume more fish than they produce: it can take three pounds of fish meal to yield one pound of salmon.

Catching More Fish

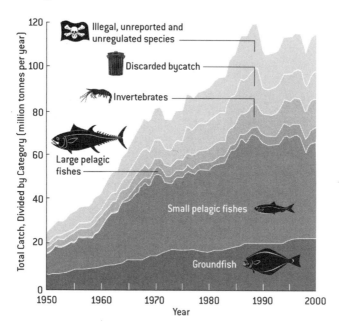

Amount of fish landed has more than quintupled over the past 50 years. As the world's population has grown, commercial fishing technology has advanced, and demand for fish in some countries has surged.

One approach to resolving the difficulties now besetting the world's fisheries is ecosystem-based management, which would seek to maintain—or, where necessary, reestablish—the structure and function of the ecosystems within which fisheries are embedded. This would involve considering the food requirements of key species in ecosystems (notably those of marine mammals), phasing out fishing gear that destroys the sea bottom, and implementing marine reserves, or "no-take zones," to mitigate the effects of fishing. Such strategies are compatible with the set of reforms that have been proposed for years by various fisheries scientists and economists: radically reducing global fleet capacity; abolishing government subsidies that keep otherwise unprofitable fishing fleets afloat; and strictly enforcing restrictions on gear that harm habitats or that capture "bycatch," species that will ultimately be thrown away.

Creating no-take zones will be key to preserving the world's fisheries. Some refuges should be close to shore, to protect coastal species; others must be large and offshore, to shield oceanic fishes. No-take zones now exist, but they are small and scattered. Indeed, the total area protected from any form of fishing constitutes a mere 0.01 percent of the ocean surface. Reserves are now viewed by fishers—and even by governments—as necessary concessions to conservationist pressure, but they must become management tools for protecting exploited species from overfishing.

A major goal should be to conserve species that once maintained themselves at deeper depths and farther offshore, before fishers developed improved gear for going after them. This type of fishing is similar to a nonrenewable mining operation because fishes are very vulnerable, typically long-lived, and have very low productivity in the dark, cold depths. These measures would enable fisheries, for the first time, to become sustainable.

The Authors

Daniel Pauly and Reg Watson are fisheries researchers at the Sea Around Us Project in Vancouver, where Pauly is the principal investigator and Watson is a senior scientist. The project, which was initiated and funded by the Pew Charitable Trusts, is based at the Fisheries Center at the University of British Columbia and is devoted to studying the impact of fishing on marine ecosystems. Pauly's early career centered on formulating new approaches for fisheries research and management in tropical developing countries. He has designed software programs for evaluating fish stocks and initiated FishBase, the online encyclopedia of fishes of the world. Watson's interests include fisheries modeling, data visualization and computer mapping. His current research focuses on mapping the effects of global fisheries, modeling underwater visual census techniques and using computer simulations to optimize fisheries.

Changes in ocean life have prompted changes in ocean industry. As fishing has become more difficult, fish farms have become a popular way of raising seafood. Fish farmers create water conditions good for breeding and raising fish; then harvest and sell the fish for food—kind of like a fish garden.

This practice of fish farming is known as aquaculture, and it's been around for more than three decades. If not managed well, large fish farms release pollution directly into the ocean. Such pollution often includes leftover fish food and waste products, which add extra nutrients to the water. The extra nutrients help algae and other small marine plants grow rapidly, which can be toxic or suffocating to ocean fish, and have a devastating effect on the balance of life in the oceans.

About 100 marine organisms are farmed in the United States, including shrimp. The following article focuses on how worldwide shrimp farming is affecting the environment, including polluting coastal waters, potentially spreading disease, and threatening biodiversity. —KW

"Shrimp Aquaculture and the Environment" by Claude E. Boyd and Jason W. Clay
Scientific American, June 1998

Shrimp aquaculture, or farming, first became profitable during the 1970s and has since mushroomed into a widespread enterprise throughout the tropical world. Thailand, Indonesia, China, India and other Asian nations now host about 1.2 million hectares (three million acres) of shrimp ponds on their soil, and nearly 200,000 hectares of coastline in the Western Hemisphere have been similarly transformed. Though rare in the U.S., where fewer than 1,000 hectares are devoted to shrimp farming, at least 130,000 hectares of Ecuador are covered with shrimp ponds. The seafood produced in this fashion ends up almost exclusively on plates in the U.S., Europe or Japan.

Hailed as the "blue revolution" a quarter century ago, raising shrimp, like many other forms of aquaculture, appeared to offer a way to reduce the pressure that overfishing brought to bear on wild populations. Shrimp farming also promised to limit massive collateral damage that trawling for these creatures did to other marine species, 10 kilograms of marine life being caught routinely for each kilogram of shrimp taken from the sea. Unfortunately, neither of these benefits has, as of yet, fully materialized. And as the record of the past two decades of shrimp farming clearly shows, aquaculture often creates its own set of environmental problems.

Down on the Farm

Normally, shrimp mate in the ocean. A single female spawns 100,000 or more eggs at a time, and within 24 hours the eggs that are fertilized hatch into larvae, which soon start feeding on plankton. After the larval period ends (about 12 days later), the young shrimp migrate from the open ocean into nutrient-rich estuaries, where they grow into more robust juveniles. Later they return to the sea to mature and mate.

For the most part, shrimp farming attempts to duplicate this natural life cycle. Aquaculturists induce adult broodstock to spawn in hatcheries by manipulating lighting, temperature, salinity, hormonal cycles and nutrients. After the eggs hatch, the managers of the hatcheries quickly transfer the offspring to rearing tanks where they can mature. During the early stages of this process, the tiny shrimp feed on microscopic algae. After the larvae grow bigger, they receive brine shrimp and manufactured feed. The managers keep the young shrimp in rearing tanks for an additional three weeks or so before releasing them into larger ponds.

In southeast Asia, most shrimp ponds are stocked with such hatchery-produced young. But in Latin America, many shrimp farmers prefer to raise larvae caught in the wild, because they are thought to be stronger and survive better in ponds. So the price for wild progeny may be more than twice that of shrimp conceived in a hatchery, and armies of collectors take to the water with nets to capture young shrimp for sale to the farmers. It is not clear whether fishing out so many larvae has depleted populations of wild shrimp. Still, in Central America, some commercial shrimp trawlers report that their catches declined noticeably when people began collecting larvae in large numbers from nearby estuaries.

Although fishing for shrimp larvae provides much needed work for many locals, their fine-mesh nets harvest essentially everything in their path, and inadvertent taking, or "bycatch," becomes a serious problem. The statistics are difficult to verify, but some workers believe that for every young shrimp snared in the wild, 100 other marine creatures will be killed.

Other environmental problems can arise from the ponds themselves. These shallow bodies are usually built by constructing earthen embankments along their perimeter. They vary in size from a few hundred square meters to many hectares, with average depths that are typically less than two meters. Usually, shrimp farmers pump seawater into canals from where it can then flow by gravity into ponds located somewhat inland, although some small-scale operations rely on the tide for filling ponds perched close to the sea.

The location of shrimp ponds is perhaps the most critical factor in controlling their impact on the surrounding environment. In Ecuador, ponds were initially constructed on salt flats and some other areas well suited to this use. That is, they were situated in places that were not particularly important for the proper functioning of the local ecosystem or for maintaining biodiversity. Yet as these expendable lands became scarce, shrimp ponds began to invade what was, from an environmental standpoint, more valuable property—wetlands and coastal thickets of salt-tolerant mangrove trees. In Thailand and many parts of Asia, shrimp aquaculture was never limited to salt flats. Although larger operations tended to avoid mangroves, about 40 percent of the small-scale farms—facilities set up with little forethought or investment capital—displaced mangroves.

Mangroves and wetlands are extraordinarily important both for the environmental services they provide and for the many plant and animal species that depend on them. For instance, mangroves soak up excess nutrients that would otherwise pollute coastal waters, and they provide protective nurseries for young marine animals. So the estimate of the United Nations Food and Agriculture Organization that about half the world's original endowment of mangrove forest has already been lost is quite troubling.

In most countries, the destruction of mangroves is driven primarily by people seeking wood for building or for fuel. Some mangrove-lined shores, like other kinds of forests, succumb to the pressures of development, which are often greatest along the coast. Shrimp farming alone appears to be responsible for less than 10 percent of the global loss. Yet in some countries shrimp aquaculture has caused as much as 20 percent of the damage to mangroves, and in some local watersheds shrimp farming accounts for nearly all the destruction.

Intensive Care Units

There are three primary methods for raising shrimp in ponds. These systems are classified according to the density of shrimp they contain, but they differ also in the nature of the feed used and in the rate of exchange of water between the ponds and the nearby ocean.

So-called extensive systems of aquaculture raise fewer than five shrimp for each square meter of pond water, whereas intensive systems grow 20 or more shrimp for each square meter of pond. Somewhere in between are the "semi-intensive" operations. The people who manage extensive systems of aquaculture nourish their charges by treating their ponds with fertilizers or manure to promote growth of algae. No other feed is given. In contrast, pellets made from plant and fish meals, nutritional supplements and a binder to enhance the stability of the feed in the water are applied daily to ponds undergoing semi-intensive and intensive management. Production during a 100- to 120-day crop is less than 1,000 kilograms per hectare (892 pounds per acre) in extensive ponds. Semi-intensive methods might produce as much as 2,000 kilograms per hectare, and intensive cultures can, in some cases, provide a phenomenal 8,000 or more kilograms per hectare.

On average, nearly two kilograms of food are needed to produce a kilogram of shrimp. Part of the reason for the inequality is that shrimp, like other animals, are not 100 percent efficient in converting food to flesh. Also, even in the best regulated feeding systems, up to 30 percent of the feed is never consumed. Consequently, a considerable amount of waste accumulates in the ponds in the form of uneaten feed, feces, ammonia, phosphorus and carbon dioxide. Usually, no more than a quarter of the organic carbon and other nutrients provided in the feed is recovered in the fattened shrimp at harvest. The excess nutrients stimulate the growth of phytoplankton, which eventually die, sink and decompose on the bottom of the ponds, consuming large amounts of oxygen in the process.

In traditional systems of aquaculture, the operators periodically remove the unwanted nutrients, dissolved gases, phytoplankton and pathogens by flushing them out to sea. In past decades, from 10 to as much as 30 percent of the water in the ponds was disgorged into the ocean each day. Today most shrimp farmers do better, exchanging daily from 2 to 5 percent of the pond water with the sea. Some shrimp farmers are attempting to eliminate this exchange completely. They have reduced the amount of wasted feed and also kept diseases in check by taking care not to stock their ponds too densely or with any infected larvae. In intensively operated ponds, mechanical aerators inject supplemental oxygen to prevent hypoxia from harming the shrimp.

The main chemicals put into ponds are fertilizer (to stimulate the growth of plankton on which the shrimp can feed), agricultural limestone and burnt lime (for adjusting the acidity of the water and underlying soil). In Asia, shrimp farmers also routinely add porous minerals called zeolites to remove ammonia, and they sometimes dose their ponds with calcium hypochlorite, formalin and some other compounds to kill pathogens and pests.

In some areas, the pollutants released from shrimp farms have exceeded the assimilative capacities of nearby coastal waters. Even if the quality of effluents from individual ponds falls within reasonable standards, too many farms in one area will eventually overwhelm natural ecosystems nearby, frequently causing unwanted fertilization (eutrophication) of coastal waters. The problem immediately spills over to all the coastal inhabitants—including the aquaculturists themselves, who must then struggle with the contamination of their own water supply. But eutrophication is not the only threat. Viral diseases also haunt locales where concentrated shrimp aquaculture has degraded coastal waters. These diseases have sparked the collapse of much of the shrimp farming in China and Taiwan, and they have caused serious difficulties in Thailand, India and Ecuador. The pathogens at fault can travel from country to country—even from hemisphere to hemisphere—in shipments of infected hatchery-produced shrimp. Diseases of shrimp can also be spread through uncooked, processed frozen shrimp.

Shrimp farmers have learned to fight these diseases in several ways. For example, they can now test the larvae they buy from hatcheries for dangerous viruses. And they have figured out how to dispose of shrimp from infected ponds so as to contain outbreaks. Certain hatcheries are using carefully bred broodstock to ensure that the larvae they produce are disease-free. Such advances are welcome, but some shrimp farmers also turn to using medicated feeds, a tactic for combating disease that may foster the proliferation of antibiotic-resistant bacteria or otherwise upset the local microbial ecology in worrisome ways.

Running a Tighter Vessel

Shrimp aquaculturists have recently started to address environmental concerns. Many of the rules of environmental etiquette are obvious. For example, ponds should not be constructed in sandy soil (unless impermeable clay or plastic liners are used) to prevent seepage of saltwater into freshwater aquifers. Discharge of effluents into predominately freshwater bodies or onto dry land should also be prohibited. Making the proper choice of sites for the ponds is perhaps one of the easiest ways for shrimp farmers to limit environmental damage—at least for ponds that have not yet been built. There is no defense for putting shrimp ponds in mangrove forests or even in tidal wetlands. These areas are not suited for sustained shrimp farming: they often have soils that are incompatible with long-term shrimp production and, more troubling, are vulnerable to coastal storms.

Most large-scale aquaculturists have learned to do better, for themselves and for the environment, than to displace mangroves with their facilities. Instead they construct canals or pipelines to bring ocean water through the coastal mangroves to sites farther inland. And many smaller-scale shrimp farmers are forming cooperatives to pool the resources and knowledge needed for responsible operations. In Indonesia, some large producers are required by law to help small-scale shrimp farmers manage their ponds. It is imperative that such efforts expand so that shrimp farming neither causes nor takes advantage of the epidemic loss of mangroves.

Even shrimp farmers preoccupied with profitability should be able to understand the benefits of adopting better practices. It costs anywhere from $10,000 to

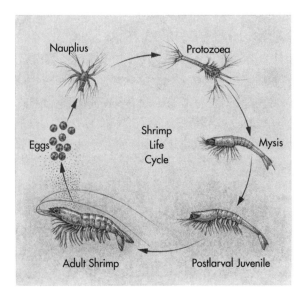

Nauplius

Protozoea

Eggs

Shrimp Life Cycle

Mysis

Adult Shrimp

Postlarval Juvenile

Shrimp life cycle (*above*), in which the eggs hatch and the shrimp grow through several stages before becoming adults, can be entirely duplicated by farmers. In the most environmentally responsible operations, shrimp are initially raised in hatchery tanks and then grown to full size in ponds that are situated well away from ecologically valuable mangrove forests. But many farmers raise young shrimp taken from the wild instead of a hatchery, and some of them build ponds where mangrove trees formerly stood, practices that risk considerable damage to the environment.

$50,000 per hectare to build proper shrimp ponds. Abandoning these works after only a few years because they have been located inappropriately not only causes considerable environmental damage, it also proves needlessly expensive. So shrimp farmers would do well to pick suitable locations away from mangroves.

And there are other simple changes that would help both the environment and the bottom line. For example, farm managers commonly broadcast large amounts of food over their ponds once or twice a day; however, many smaller feedings at more frequent intervals, combined with the use of feeding trays, would require less food and cause less waste. Improved feeds—formulations that use greater amounts of vegetable protein and less fish meal—are more digestible, appear to last longer in the water and also produce less waste. Investing in these practices would discourage overfishing of the seas for shrimp food, and it would save shrimp farmers money on feed, limit pollution and diminish the cost of cleaning up problems later. So it would also boost profits.

Another way to reduce water pollution is to avoid stocking ponds with too many juveniles and to restrict the amount of water exchanged with the sea. When the density of shrimp is right, natural processes within the ponds will assimilate much of the waste into the underlying soil. And although current technology requires ponds to be drained for harvest, operators could easily pass the water through settlement ponds to encourage denitrification and to remove many other pollutants associated with the suspended solids. Shrimp farmers should also refrain from mixing freshwater with the seawater in the ponds to reduce salinity. This practice (which, thankfully, has been abandoned by almost all shrimp farmers) is unnecessary and should be prohibited to avoid excessive drain on freshwater supplies.

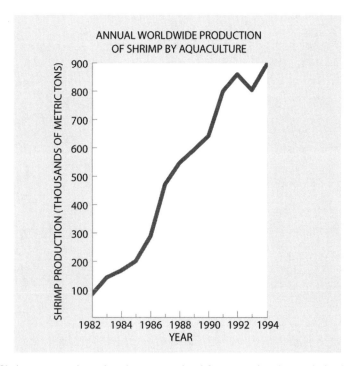

ANNUAL WORLDWIDE PRODUCTION
OF SHRIMP BY AQUACULTURE

Shrimp aquaculture has been practiced for centuries, but only in the past two decades have people raised shrimp in massive quantities (*above*). The top shrimp-producing nations straddle the equator in Asia and the Americas.

Addressing threats to biodiversity is more difficult. But many problems could be eliminated if farmers raised only shrimp procured from hatcheries, carefully regulated the importation of broodstock and young shrimp, and cultured only native species. They could also prevent larger aquatic animals from being caught in their pumps by using intake screens.

Shrimp farmers should also pay more attention to the chemical additives they employ. Although most of the chemicals used in shrimp farming have a history of safe use, the application of chemicals other than agricultural limestone, burnt lime and fertilizers is usually unnecessary. In those rare instances where antibiotics are required, government regulators should evaluate the chemicals employed and prohibit potentially harmful ones—or at least make sure that they are used in a safe manner.

These governments should also require that careful studies of environmental and social impact precede the construction of new shrimp farms. That way, the communities involved could gauge the likelihood of damage to the local environment and identify conflicts in the use of land and water. Governments must also find ways to ensure that these initial efforts to protect the environment remain effective over time.

Although environmental impact studies would be valuable for new projects, many existing shrimp farmers will clearly need to change their practices. Here both a carrot and a stick are necessary. Some shrimp producers will see the wisdom of adopting more sustainable approaches themselves. In some instances, however, governments must impose regulations.

In all, shrimp farmers should welcome the changes on the horizon. Technological innovations promise to aid them in reducing the discharge of wastewater and extending the life of their ponds. Better breeding programs should offer varieties of shrimp with greater resistance to disease. The adoption of better practices will cost producers somewhat more in the short term.

But in the long run these changes will pay for themselves by improving the efficiency and durability of their operations.

The shrimp industry seems to be responding to criticisms from environmentalists, and we are hopeful that shrimp aquaculture will prove much less harmful to the environment in the future. In fact, many of today's operations are better than those of the recent past in this regard. Yet the shrimp industry as a whole still has to evolve substantially before it attains standards that might allow shrimp aquaculture to flourish on the same site indefinitely. Only at that point will shrimp aquaculture join most other kinds of farming in achieving widespread acceptance.

Notes from an Adviser to the Shrimp Industry

It cannot be denied that a great deal of environmental damage has arisen from poor planning and management by shrimp farmers and lax government agencies in countries where this form of aquaculture is widespread. But shrimp farming is not always harmful to the environment. Unfortunately, some environmentalists have unfairly made sweeping condemnations of the entire industry.

One charge leveled against shrimp farming is that rich investors make quick profits and then abandon farms. Here the critics are just plain wrong. Although some shrimp farms have proved unsustainable and been abandoned, these farms usually were small, often consisting of only one or two cheaply constructed ponds, which were situated on unsuitable sites and operated without sufficient capital and expertise. Properly sited and well-constructed shrimp farms cost from $10,000 to $50,000 per hectare of pond and are expensive to operate. Such large investments cannot be recovered quickly, so owners want to make sure that their farms are productive for many years.

Shrimp farming is an interesting example of a situation in which a disproportionate amount of the environmental damage has resulted from smaller operators rather than from bigger ones. But it is possible for small-scale farmers to pool their resources in cooperatives or producer associations and greatly improve their management. Well-run operations require many workers up and down the line—for hatcheries, farms and processing plants—typically creating one or two jobs for each hectare of pond in production. Shrimp farming also stimulates local economies and provides import earnings for many developing nations.

So it would be a sad loss for many people if shrimp aquaculture disappeared. The trick is to manage these operations sensibly. Many shrimp farmers are, in fact, acutely aware of the damage that shrimp farming can do. They have learned that their long-term success depends on maintaining healthy conditions for their

continued on following page

continued from previous page

shrimp and that their prosperity is linked directly to environmental quality along nearby coasts. Degradation of the coastal zone makes aquaculture more difficult, so it is easy to convince most shrimp farmers that they have a vested interest in being good environmental stewards.

Several recent developments indicate that shrimp farmers are indeed moving toward "environmentally friendly" forms of production. The Australian Prawn Farmers Association established a formal code of practice for its members; the Association of Southeast Asian Nations Fisheries Network published a manual of good shrimp farm procedures; and the Food and Agriculture Organization of the United Nations presented technical guidelines for responsible fisheries that apply to shrimp farming. In addition, the Network of Aquaculture Centers in Asia-Pacific has created a detailed plan to improve the sustainability of aquaculture in general.

What is more, several recent scientific and trade meetings have focused on the connection between shrimp farming and the environment. Most countries now require environmental impact assessments for new shrimp farms. Thailand has instituted regulations in an effort to make sure that shrimp farmers adopt the best management practices possible. A particularly important development is the recent formation of the Global

Aquaculture Alliance. This industry group is fostering responsible shrimp aquaculture, developing an elaborate code of practice and promoting consumer awareness with an "eco-label" for environmentally friendly shrimp.

—*Claude E. Boyd*

Comments from an Environmental Advocate

Many businesspeople see natural resources as free for the taking. They count as costs only the labor and investment to extract them. There is no thought given to the cost of replacement or maintenance for the resources they use. Nowhere is this blindness more true than with shrimp aquaculturists, who often depend on access to public resources that, traditionally, have been used by many different groups.

Shrimp farmers must decide if they indeed want to address the environmental problems their industry has created. True, all economic activities have environmental consequences. Nevertheless, the goal of shrimp producers should be to reduce the deleterious effects on the environment as much as possible.

Some practices that would make shrimp farming more sustainable are already used by more progressive and well-financed shrimp producers. Around the world,

continued on following page

continued from previous page

however, there are hundreds of thousands of shrimp farmers. Each one makes decisions that affect his or her own future as well as those of others in this business. Shrimp aquaculture as it is conducted today in most parts of the world is not sustainable for very many decades into the future.

Perhaps an ideal, indefinitely sustainable system for shrimp farming is not possible, at least with current knowledge. Yet most shrimp farmers and others affected by this industry could agree that some practices are better than others, and the industry as a whole would benefit from the swift adoption of these improved techniques.

There are a number of business reasons to adopt more efficient and sustainable methods of shrimp production. For example, increasing the survival rates of young shrimp from less than 50 to 75 percent or more will reduce the initial outlays required for each crop. Similarly, more effective ways of feeding shrimp can reduce expenditures on food by a quarter to a half. These two simple changes would reduce the cost of cleaning effluents and moving ponds periodically. Ecuadorian shrimp farmers have been able to double their profits by such means.

Although other improvements may be more expensive, the boost to income in many instances will compensate for the required expenditures. Yet it is important to understand that some investments will not result in increased efficiency. These costs will have to be passed on to consumers, who are, after all, the ultimate polluters in the economic system. Regulations might bring increased prices. Or perhaps "green" shrimp will prove to command a premium from environmentally conscious consumers.

But producers who try to differentiate their product to gain market advantage must be able to prove their claims. People will pay more only if a reliable third party has verified assertions about the product being environmentally benign. Because there are no "name brands" of shrimp, such assurances will be difficult to judge.

Who should establish the guidelines for sustainable shrimp production? Today environmentalists, producers and some governments are each developing their own guidelines for sustainable shrimp aquaculture. But no single group, certainly not the producers themselves, will be able to create a credible system. Attaining that goal will require that these diverse groups agree on general principles, which can then be adapted to specific local conditions. Only through the adoption of such sustainable production systems will shrimp aquaculture be part of the solution for the next millennium rather than just another environmental problem that must be put right. —*Jason W. Clay*

The Authors

Claude E. Boyd and Jason W. Clay can represent widely differing perspectives on shrimp aquaculture with good authority. Boyd received a Ph.D. in water and aquatic soil chemistry from Auburn University in Alabama in 1966 and is currently a professor there in the department of fisheries and allied aquacultures. He also works regularly as an adviser for shrimp aquaculturists around the globe. Clay obtained a Ph.D. in anthropology and international agriculture from Cornell University in 1979. Now a senior research fellow at the World Wildlife Fund in Washington, D.C., Clay has taught at Harvard University, conducted social science analysis for the U.S. Department of Agriculture and has served as the director of research for Cultural Survival, a human-rights organization working with indigenous peoples throughout the world.

Changes in ocean life can actually make seafood-eating humans sick. When ocean conditions are just right, populations of small marine plants called phytoplankton grow. These plentiful plants are then eaten by shellfish, including clams and mussels. A few dozen species of phytoplankton are toxic to humans, and when these populations grow rapidly, they can build up in shellfish and cause diarrhea, memory loss, and even death to humans when eaten in large quantities.

Such phytoplankton population spikes are called red tides (because they sometimes turn coastal waters red), and scientists are still trying to figure out what causes them. Because there are so many different types of phytoplankton that can create red tides, scientists say it's hard to make definitive conclusions.

Many scientists believe red tides have become more common in the last couple of decades. Is it just coincidence? Is it simply the result of increased scientific awareness of the tides? Or is it due to pollution or other human activities? No one knows for sure. This article explores what we know about red tides and why we should pay attention. —KW

"Red Tides"
by Donald M. Anderson
Scientific American, August 1994

Late in 1987 scientists faced a baffling series of marine catastrophes. First, 14 humpback whales died in Cape Cod Bay, Mass., during a five-week period. This die-off, equivalent to 50 years of "natural" mortality, was not a stranding, in which healthy whales beach themselves. Instead the cetaceans died at sea—some rapidly—and then washed ashore. Postmortem examinations showed that the whales had been well immediately before their deaths and that many of them had abundant blubber and fish in their stomachs, evidence of recent feeding. Alarmed and saddened, the public and press blamed pollution or a chemical spill for the mysterious deaths.

Two more mass poisonings occurred that month, but the victims in these new cases were humans. Fishermen and beachgoers along the North Carolina coast started complaining of respiratory problems and eye irritation. Within days, residents and visitors who had eaten local shellfish experienced diarrhea, dizziness and other symptoms suggesting neurotoxic poisoning. The illnesses bewildered epidemiologists and even prompted public conjecture that a nearby sunken submarine was leaking poison gas.

Concurrently, hospitals in Canada began admitting patients suffering from disorientation, vomiting, diarrhea and abdominal cramps. All had eaten mussels from Prince Edward Island. Although Canadian authorities had dealt with shellfish poisoning outbreaks for decades, these symptoms were unfamiliar and disturbing: some patients exhibited permanent short-term memory loss. They could remember addresses but could not recall their most recent meal, for example. The officials quickly restricted the sale and distribution of mussels but eventually reported three deaths and 105 cases of acute poisoning in humans.

We now know that these seemingly unrelated events were all caused, either directly or indirectly, by toxic, single-celled algae called phytoplankton—vast blooms of which are commonly referred to as red tides.

Although red tides have been recorded throughout history, the incidents mentioned above were entirely unexpected. As we shall see, they illustrate several major issues that have begun to challenge the scientific and regulatory communities.

Indeed, there is a conviction among many experts that the scale and complexity of this natural phenomenon are expanding. They note that the number of toxic blooms, the economic losses from them, the types of resources affected and the kinds of toxins and toxic species have all increased. Is this expansion real? Is it a global epidemic, as some claim? Is it related to human activities, such as rising coastal pollution? Or is it a result of increased scientific awareness and improved surveillance or analytical capabilities? To address these issues, we must understand the physiological, toxicological and ecological mechanisms underlying the growth and proliferation of red tide algae and the manner in which they cause harm.

Certain blooms of algae are termed red tides when the tiny pigmented plants grow in such abundance that they change the color of the seawater to red, brown or even green. The name is misleading, however, because many toxic events are called red tides even when the waters show no discoloration. Likewise, an accumulation of nontoxic, harmless algae can change the color of ocean water. The picture is even more complicated: some phytoplankton neither discolor the water nor produce toxins but kill marine animals in other ways. Many diverse phenomena thus fall under the "red tide" rubric.

Of the thousands of living phytoplankton species that make up the base of the marine food web, only a few dozen are known to be toxic. Most are dinoflagellates, prymnesiophytes or chloromonads. A bloom develops when these single-celled algae photosynthesize and multiply, converting dissolved nutrients and sunlight into plant biomass. The dominant mode of reproduction is simple asexual fission—one cell grows larger, then divides into two cells, the two split into four, and so on. Barring a shortage of nutrients or light, or heavy grazing by tiny zooplankton that consume the algae, the population's size can increase rapidly. In some cases, a milliliter of seawater can contain tens or hundreds of thousands of algal cells. Spread over large areas, the phenomenon can be both visually spectacular and catastrophic.

Some species switch to sexual reproduction when nutrients are scarce. They form thick-walled, dormant cells, called cysts, that settle on the seafloor and can survive there for years. When favorable growth conditions return, cysts germinate and reinoculate the water with swimming cells that can then bloom. Although not all red tide species form cysts, many do, and this transformation explains important aspects of their ecology and biogeography. The timing and location of a bloom can depend on when the cysts germinate and where they were deposited, respectively. Cyst production facilitates species dispersal as well; blooms carried into new waters by currents or other means can deposit "seed" populations to colonize previously unaffected areas.

A dramatic example of natural dispersal occurred in 1972, when a massive red tide reaching from Maine to Massachusetts followed a September hurricane. The shellfish toxicity detected then for the first time has recurred in that region virtually every year now for two decades. The cyst stage has provided a very effective strategy for the survival and dispersal of many other red tide species as well.

How do algal blooms cause harm? One of the most serious impacts on human life occurs when clams, mussels, oysters or scallops ingest the algae as food and retain the toxins in their tissues. Typically the shellfish themselves are only marginally affected, but a single clam can sometimes accumulate enough toxin to kill a human being. These shellfish poisoning syndromes have been described as paralytic, diarrhetic and neurotoxic, shortened to PSP, DSP and NSP. The 1987 Canadian outbreak in which some patients suffered memory loss was appropriately characterized as amnesic shellfish poisoning, or ASP. The North Carolina episode was NSP.

A related problem, ciguatera fish poisoning, or CFP, causes more human illness than any other kind of toxicity originating in seafood. It occurs predominantly in tropical and subtropical islands, where from 10,000 to 50,000 individuals may be affected annually. Dinoflagellates that live attached to seaweeds produce the ciguatera toxins. Herbivorous fishes eat the seaweeds and the attached dinoflagellates as well. Because ciguatera toxin is soluble in fat, it is stored in the fishes' tissues and travels through the food web to carnivores. The most dangerous fish to eat are thus the largest and oldest, often considered the most desirable as well.

Symptoms do vary among the different syndromes but are generally neurological or gastrointestinal, or both. DSP causes diarrhea, nausea and vomiting, whereas PSP symptoms include tingling and numbness of the mouth, lips and fingers, accompanied by general muscular weakness. Acute doses inhibit respiration, and death results from respiratory paralysis. NSP triggers diarrhea, vomiting and abdominal pain, followed by muscular aches, dizziness, anxiety, sweating and peripheral tingling. Ciguatera induces an intoxication syndrome nearly identical to NSP.

Illnesses and deaths from algal-derived shellfish poisons vary in number from year to year and from country to country. Environmental fluctuations profoundly influence the growth and accumulation of algae and thus their toxicity as well. Furthermore, countries differ in their ability to monitor shellfish and detect biotoxins before they reach the market. Developed countries typically operate monitoring programs that permit the timely closure of contaminated resources. Illnesses and deaths are thus rare, unless a new toxin appears (as in the ASP crisis in Canada) or an outbreak occurs in an area with no history of the problem (as in North Carolina). Developing countries, especially those having long coastlines or poor populations who rely primarily on the sea for food, are more likely to incur a higher incidence of sickness and death from algal blooms.

Phytoplankton can also kill marine animals directly. In the Gulf of Mexico, the dinoflagellate *Gymnodinium breve* frequently causes devastating fish kills. As the wild fish swim through *G. breve* blooms, the fragile algae rupture, releasing neurotoxins onto the gills of the fish. Within a short time, the animals asphyxiate. Tons of dead fish sometimes cover the beaches along Florida's Gulf Coast, causing several millions of dollars to be lost in tourism and other recreation based-businesses.

Farmed fish are especially vulnerable because the caged animals cannot avoid the blooms. Each year, farmed salmon, yellowtail and other economically important species fall victim to a variety of algal species. Blooms can wipe out entire fish farms within hours, killing fingerlings and large fish alike. Algal blooms thus pose a large threat to fish farms and their insurance providers. In Norway an extensive program is underway to minimize these impacts. Fish farmers make weekly observations of algal concentrations and water clarity. Other parameters are transmitted to shore from instruments on moored buoys. The Norwegian Ministry of Environment then combines this information with a five-day weather forecast to generate an "algal forecast" for fish farmers and authorities. Fish cages in peril are then towed to clear water.

Unfortunately, not much more can be done. The ways in which algae kill fish are poorly understood.

Some phytoplankton species produce polyunsaturated fatty acids and galactolipids that destroy blood cells. Such an effect would explain the ruptured gills, hypoxia and edema in dying fish. Other algal species produce these hemolytic compounds and neurotoxins as well. The combination can significantly reduce a fish's heart rate, resulting in reduced blood flow and a deadly decrease in oxygen.

Moreover, nontoxic phytoplankton can kill fish. The diatom genus *Chaetoceros* has been linked to dying salmon in the Puget Sound area of Washington State, yet no toxin has ever been identified in this group. Instead species such as *C. convolutus* sport long, barbed spines that lodge between gill tissues and trigger the release of massive amounts of mucus. Continuous irritation exhausts the supply of mucus and mucous cells, causing lamellar degeneration and death from reduced oxygen exchange. These barbed spines probably did not evolve specifically to kill fish, since only caged fish succumb to the blooms. The problems faced by fish farmers are more likely the unfortunate result of an evolutionary strategy by certain *Chaetoceros* species to avoid predation or to stay afloat.

Algal toxins also cause mortalities as they move through the marine food web. Some years ago tons of herring died in the Bay of Fundy after consuming small planktonic snails that had eaten the PSP-producing dinoflagellate *Alexandrium*. From the human health standpoint, it is fortunate that herring, cod, salmon and other commercial fish are sensitive to these toxins and, unlike shellfish, die before toxins reach dangerous levels in their flesh. Some toxin, however, accumulates in the liver and other organs of certain fish, and so animals such as other fish, marine mammals and birds that consume whole fish, including the viscera, are at risk.

We now can reconstruct the events that killed the whales in 1987. A few weeks of intense investigations that year by marine pathologist Joseph R. Geraci of the Ontario Veterinary College, myself and many others revealed that the PSP toxins most likely caused these deaths. The dinoflagellate *Alexandrium tamarense* produced the toxins, which reached the whales via their food web. We analyzed mackerel that the whales had been eating and found saxitoxin, not in their flesh but concentrated in the liver and kidney. Presumably the mackerel ate zooplankton and small fish that had previously dined on *Alexandrium*.

The humpbacks were starting their southward migration and were feeding heavily. Assuming that they consumed 4 percent of their body weight daily, we calculated that they received a saxitoxin dosage of 3.2 micrograms per kilogram of body weight. But was this a fatal dose? Unfortunately, in 1987 we had no data that directly addressed how much toxin would kill a whale. We knew the minimum lethal dose of saxitoxin for humans is seven to 16 micrograms per kilogram of body weight, but that was two to five times more than what the whales had probably ingested.

Our calculations were initially disheartening, but as we thought about it we realized that whales might be more sensitive to the toxins than are humans. First, whales would have received continual doses of toxin as they fed, whereas human mortality statistics are based on single feedings. Second, during a dive, the mammalian diving reflex channels blood and oxygen predominantly to the heart and brain. The same mechanism sometimes protects young children who fall through thin ice and survive drowning, despite being underwater for half an hour or longer. For humans, cold water induces the reflex, but for whales, it is activated during every dive.

Each dive then would expose the most sensitive organs to the toxin, which would bypass the liver and kidney, where it could be metabolized and excreted. Finally, saxitoxin need not have killed the whales directly. Even a slightly incapacitated animal might have difficulty orienting to the water surface or breathing correctly. The whales may actually have drowned following a sub-lethal exposure to saxitoxin. The exact cause will never be known, but the evidence strongly suggests that these magnificent creatures died from a natural toxin originating in microscopic algae.

Other examples of toxins traveling up the food web appear nearly every year. In 1991 sick or dying brown pelicans and cormorants were found near Monterey Bay, Calif. Wildlife experts could find no signs that pesticides, heavy metals or other pollutants were involved. The veterinarian in charge of the study telephoned Jeffrey Wright of the National Research Council laboratory in Halifax, Nova Scotia. Wright had directed the Canadian Mussel Toxin Crisis Team that identified the poison responsible for the mysterious ASP episode in1987. His team had isolated a toxin from the Prince Edward Island mussels, called domoic acid, and traced it to its source—a diatom, *Pseudonitzschia pungens*, that had been considered harmless. Four years later members of the same Canadian team quickly ascertained that the sick and dying birds in California had eaten anchovies that contained domoic acid, again from Pseudonitzschia (but a different species).

The toxins responsible for these syndromes are not single chemical entities but are families of compounds having similar chemical structures and effects. For example, the saxitoxins that cause PSP are a family of at least 18 different compounds with widely differing potencies. Most algal toxins cause human illness by disrupting electrical conduction, uncoupling communication between nerve and muscle, and impeding critical physiological processes. To do so, they bind to specific membrane receptors, leading to changes in the intracellular concentration of ions such as sodium or calcium.

 The saxitoxins bind to sodium channels and block the flux of sodium in and out of nerve and muscle cells. Brevetoxins, the family of nine compounds responsible for NSP, bind to a different site on the sodium channel but cause the opposite effect from saxitoxin. Domoic acid disrupts normal neurochemical transmission in the brain. It binds to kainate receptors in the central nervous system, causing a sustained depolarization of the neurons and eventually cell degeneration and death. Memory loss in ASP victims apparently results from lesions in the hippocampus, where kainate receptors abound.

Why do algal species produce toxins? Some argue that toxins evolved as a defense mechanism against zooplankton and other grazers. Indeed, some zooplankton can become slowly incapacitated while feeding, as though they are being gradually paralyzed or otherwise impaired. (In one study, a tintinnid ciliate could swim only backward, away from its intended prey, after exposure to toxic dinoflagellates.) Sometimes grazing animals spit out the toxic algae as though they had an unpleasant taste. These responses would all reduce grazing and thus facilitate bloom formation.

All the same, nontoxic phytoplankton also form blooms, and so it is unlikely that toxins serve solely as self-defense. Scientists are looking within the algae for biochemical pathways that require the toxins, but the search thus far has been fruitless. The toxins are not proteins, and all are synthesized in a series of chemical steps requiring multiple genes. Investigators have proposed biosynthetic pathways, but they have not isolated chemical intermediates or enzymes used only in toxin production. It has thus been difficult to apply the powerful tools of molecular biology to these organisms, other than to study their genes or to develop detection tools.

We do have some tantalizing clues about toxin metabolism. For example, certain dinoflagellate strains produce different amounts of toxin and different sets of toxin derivatives when we vary their growth conditions. Metabolism of the toxins is a dynamic process, but we still do not know whether they have a specific biochemical role. As with the spiny diatoms that kill fish, the illnesses and mortalities caused by algal "toxins" may be the result of the accidental chemical affinity of those metabolites for receptor sites on ion channels in higher animals.

The potential role of bacteria or bacterial genes in phytoplankton toxin production is an area of active research. We wonder how a genetically diverse array of organisms, including phytoplankton, seaweeds, bacteria and cyanobacteria, could all have evolved the genes needed to produce saxitoxin. Several years ago Masaaki Kodama of Kitasato University in Japan isolated intracellular bacteria from antibiotic treated *A. tamarense* cultures and showed that the bacteria produced saxitoxin. This finding supported an old and long ignored hypothesis that toxins might originate from bacteria living inside or on the dinoflagellate cell.

Despite considerable study, the jury is still out. Many scientists now accept that some bacteria produce saxitoxins, but they point out that dense bacterial cultures produce extremely small quantities. It is also not clear that those bacteria can be found inside dinoflagellates. That intracellular bacteria produce all of the toxin found in a dinoflagellate cell therefore seems unlikely, but perhaps some synergism occurs between a small number of symbionts and the host dinoflagellate that is lost when the bacteria are isolated in culture. Alternatively, a bacterial gene or plasmid might be involved.

Given the diverse array of algae that produce toxins or cause problems in a variety of oceanographic systems, attempts to generalize the dynamics of harmful algal blooms are doomed to fail. Many harmful species, however, share some mechanisms. Red tides often occur when heating or freshwater runoff creates a stratified surface layer above colder, nutrient-rich waters. Fast-growing algae quickly strip away nutrients in the upper layer, leaving nitrogen and phosphorus only below the interface of the layers, called the pycnocline. Nonmotile phytoplankton cannot easily get to this layer, whereas motile algae, including dinoflagellates, can thrive. Many swim at speeds in excess of 10 meters per day, and some undergo daily vertical migration: they reside in surface waters by day to harvest sunlight like sunbathers, then swim down to the pycnocline to take up nutrients at night. As a result, blooms can suddenly appear in surface waters that are devoid of nutrients and would seem incapable of supporting such prolific growth.

A similar sleight-of-hand can occur horizontally, though over much larger distances. The NSP outbreak in North Carolina illustrates how ocean currents can transport major toxic species from one area to another.

Patricia A. Tester, a biologist at the National Oceanic and Atmospheric Administration's National Marine Fisheries Service laboratory in Beaufort, examined plankton from local waters under a microscope soon after the initial reports of human illnesses. She saw cells resembling the dinoflagellate *G. breve*, the cause of recurrent NSP along Florida's western coast. Experts quickly confirmed her tentative identification, and for the first time in state history, authorities closed shellfish beds because of algal toxins, resulting in a loss of $20 million.

Tester and her coworkers have since used satellite images of sea-surface temperatures to argue that the *G. breve* population in North Carolina originated off the southwestern coast of Florida, nearly 1,000 kilometers away. That bloom traveled from the Gulf of Mexico up the southeastern coast of the U.S., transported by several current systems culminating in the Gulf Stream. After 30 days of transport, a filament of water separated from the Gulf Stream and moved onto North Carolina's narrow continental shelf, carrying *G. breve* cells with it. The warm water mass remained in nearshore waters, identifiable in satellite images for three weeks. Fortunately, *G. breve* does not have a known cyst stage, so it could not establish a seedbed and colonize this new region.

This incident, taken together with many others like it throughout the world, speaks of an unsettling trend. Problems from harmful red tides have grown worse over the past two decades. The causes, however, are multiple, and only some relate to pollution or other human activities. For example, the global expansion in aquaculture means that more areas are monitored closely, and more fisheries' products that can be killed or take up toxins are in the water. Likewise, our discovery of toxins in algal species formerly considered nontoxic reflects the maturation of this field of science, now profiting from more investigators, better analytical techniques and chemical instrumentation, and more efficient communication among workers.

Long-term studies at the local or regional level do show that red tides (in the most general sense of the term) are increasing as coastal pollution worsens. Between 1976 and 1986, as the population around Tolo Harbor in Hong Kong grew sixfold, red tides increased eightfold. Pollution presumably provided more nutrients to the algae. A similar pattern emerged in the Inland Sea of Japan, where visible red tides proliferated steadily from 44 per year in 1965 to more than 300 a decade later. Japanese authorities instituted rigorous effluent controls in the mid-1970s, and a 50 percent reduction in the number of red tides ensued.

These examples have been criticized, since both could be biased by changes in the numbers of observers through time, and both are tabulations of water discolorations from blooms, not just toxic or harmful episodes. Still, the data demonstrate what should be an obvious relationship: coastal waters receiving industrial, agricultural and domestic waste, frequently rich in plant nutrients, should experience a general increase in algal growth. These nutrients can enhance toxic or harmful episodes in several ways. Most simply, all phytoplankton species, toxic and nontoxic, benefit, but we notice the enrichment of toxic ones more. Fertilize your lawn, and you get more grass—and more dandelions.

Some scientists propose instead that pollution selectively stimulates harmful species. Theodore J. Smayda of the University of Rhode Island brings the nutrient ratio hypothesis, an old concept in the scientific literature, to bear on toxic bloom phenomena. He argues that human activities have altered the relative availability of specific nutrients in coastal waters in ways that favor toxic forms. For example, diatoms, most of which are harmless, require silicon in their cell walls, whereas other phytoplankton do not. Because silicon is not abundant in sewage, but nitrogen and phosphorus are, the ratio of nitrogen to silicon or of phosphorus to silicon in coastal waters has increased over the past several decades. Diatom growth ceases when silicon supplies are depleted, but other phytoplankton classes, which often include more toxic species, can proliferate using "excess" nitrogen and phosphorus. This idea is controversial but not unfounded. A 23-year time series from the German coast documents a fourfold rise in the nitrogen-silicon and phosphorus-silicon ratios, accompanied by a striking change in the composition of the phytoplankton community: diatoms decreased, whereas flagellates increased more than 10-fold.

Another concern is the long-distance transport of algal species in cargo vessels. We have long recognized that ships carry marine organisms in their ballast water, but evidence is emerging that toxic algae have also been hitchhiking across the oceans. Gustaaf M. Hallegraeff of the University of Tasmania has frequently donned a miner's helmet and ventured into the bowels of massive cargo ships to sample sediments accumulated in ballast tanks. He found more than 300 million toxic dinoflagellate cysts in one vessel alone. Hallegraeff argues that one PSP-producing dinoflagellate species first appeared in Tasmanian waters during the past two decades, concurrent with the development of a local woodchip industry. Empty vessels that begin a journey in a foreign harbor pump water and sediment into their tanks for ballast; when wood chips are loaded in Tasmania, the tanks are discharged. Cysts easily survive the transit cruise and colonize the new site. Australia has now issued strict guidelines for discharging ballast water in the country's ports. Unfortunately, most other nations do not have such restrictions.

The past decade may be remembered as the time that humankind's effect on the global environment caught the public eye in a powerful and ominous fashion. For some, signs of our neglect come with forecasts of global warming, deforestation or decreases in biodiversity. For me and my colleagues, this interval brought a bewildering expansion in the complexity and scale of the red tide phenomenon. The signs are clear that pollution has enhanced the abundance of algae, including harmful and toxic forms. This effect is obvious in Hong Kong and the Inland Sea of Japan and is perhaps real but less evident in regions where coastal pollution is more gradual and unobtrusive. But we cannot blame all new outbreaks and new problems on pollution. There are many other factors that contribute to the proliferation of toxic species; some involve human activities, and some do not. Nevertheless, we may well be witnessing a sign that should not be ignored. As a growing world population demands more and more of fisheries' resources, we must respect our coastal waters and minimize those activities that stimulate the spectacular and destructive outbreaks called red tides.

The Author

Donald M. Anderson is a Senior Scientist at the Woods Hole Oceanographic Institution. In 1977 he earned a doctorate in aquatic sciences from the department of civil engineering at the Massachusetts Institute of Technology. Anderson studies the physiological and genetic regulation of toxicity in dinoflagellates, their bloom dynamics and the global biogeography of toxic Alexandrium *species. He also participates in various international programs for cooperative research and training on red tides, marine biotoxins and harmful algae.*

Changes in ocean life have made fishermen more aware of what they catch. In the Atlantic Ocean off the northeast coast of the United States, fishermen use nets to scoop up whatever fish are in the area. Using this method, they often catch and kill creatures accidentally, including harbor porpoises.

The following article is about early research to scare porpoises away from fishing nets using little noisemakers called pingers. When they were first used in the early 1990s, pingers appeared to keep porpoises from being accidentally caught in nets—a good thing. But if the sound scares porpoises away, scientists want to know if it harms other marine life—a bad thing.

Understanding effects of underwater sound on marine life is a touchy subject—and a hot research topic. Today, small acoustic pingers are manufactured and sold commercially. We know these sorts of devices—plus the sound from ships, recreation, and military activities at sea—make the oceans a very noisy place. What we don't know is how marine animals respond to the noise. —KW

"Alarming Nets"
by David Schneider
Scientific American, September 1996

In search of a fish dinner, harbor porpoises range quite close to shore. Unfortunately, that behavior can send the creatures into the nets of commercial fishermen plying the same waters. In New England the death of harbor porpoises in nets set along the bottom seemed so rampant that wildlife conservationists petitioned the federal government in 1991 to designate the local population as officially threatened. That move would have severely restricted fishing in the region. But instead of challenging the porpoise advocates in court, some fishermen joined with scientists, engineers and environmentalists to find a technical solution. That effort resulted in an underwater acoustic alarm—a "pinger"—that keeps the porpoises from entangling themselves. Yet, despite tests that have shown the efficacy of these devices, many scientists have remained frustratingly slow in blessing the pingers.

The problem stemmed from a general belief among marine biologists that acoustic deterrents were ineffective. An influential review article published in 1991 in *Marine Mammal Science* stated flatly that "studies undertaken to determine whether sound emitters reduce entanglement have been inconclusive, and have so far failed to demonstrate better than a marginal reduction in entanglement rates, if any."

But some fishermen, scientists and environmentalists felt otherwise. "We had been blinded by the literature that said it didn't work," admits Scott D. Kraus, a marine biologist at the New England Aquarium in Boston. Nevertheless, some members of an informal "harbor porpoise working group" decided to approach Jon Lien, a professor of animal behavior at

Memorial University in St. Johns, Newfoundland, who had been using acoustic devices to prevent whales from colliding with fishing gear.

With their first attempt at using Lien's pingers in 1992, the fishermen saw a remarkable reduction in the entanglement of harbor porpoises. Whereas a set of control nets without pingers snared 10 harbor porpoises, the nets set with Lien's sounders entangled none. Yet naysayers complained that the fishermen had placed the pingers in areas they knew would be free from porpoise traffic.

So with $9,000 from the U.S. National Marine Fisheries Service, Lien and the New England fishermen mounted a more elaborate experiment in 1993, using new pingers that they constructed on the spot. "We went to Radio Shack and got a sound generator and went to a hardware store and got some plumbing," Lien recalls. They also deployed their test nets in an arrangement that kept the control nets in proximity, avoiding the possibility of experimenter bias. Again the results were positive. Nets fully outfitted with pingers trapped only one harbor porpoise; those without caught 32 of the animals.

But critics once more found reason to question the experiment, noting that some of the harbor porpoises had been trapped close to the juncture between pinger-studded and pinger-free sides. A panel of experts convened by the National Marine Fisheries Service determined that the fishermen's experiments, though promising, were inconclusive.

Only a large-scale, statistically controlled experiment would produce a definitive answer. So the porpoise working group appealed to Congress for the necessary funds. Their lobbying efforts included a refreshing twist: the fishermen in the group argued on behalf of the endangered porpoises, and the environmentalists present argued on behalf of the endangered New England fishermen. That tactic startled Congress into approving a large scale study.

During their 1994 trials, the group monitored more than 10,000 fishing nets, each as long as a football field. To rule out any possibility of bias, all the nets were fitted with pingers, but only half of them had sounders that were operative. Special switches powered up the devices after they were cast overboard, and thus the participants could not distinguish live pingers from duds while deploying the nets.

As the experiment progressed, it soon became clear that the pingers were deterring porpoises. In the final count, 25 porpoises became entangled in the control nets, whereas only two suffered in an equal number of nets outfitted with working pingers—and one of those animals was most likely deaf. Moreover, the acoustic beacons did not scare away the desired fish.

The New England fishermen are now even more confident that the harbor porpoise problem can be solved with pingers. Some scientists and conservationists, however, remain cautious. David N. Wiley, a senior scientist with the International Wildlife Coalition in Massachusetts, for example, warns that the pingers "have not been shown to be without detrimental 'side effects'. . . ." Other scientists question how effective the pingers will prove to be during different seasons and over long periods.

But like doctors who have observed positive results in clinical trials, the fishermen are reluctant to continue running tests. And they wonder why some scientists and government regulators have been so slow to pay attention to pingers—something even porpoises seem able to do.

3 | Changes in Ocean Temperature

Changes in ocean temperature could cause sea level to rise. This is because the temperature of the water, like most substances, actually affects how much space the ocean takes up. When water gets warm it expands—filling more space. Think of what a pot of water does when it boils—it often expands and spills over the sides.

While no one is predicting that the ocean will boil over, scientists say even a small warming and expansion of seawater could potentially flood coastal communities. Today, most scientists agree that sea level has been rising by a couple millimeters a year for the past several decades.

Of special interest is whether ice at the North and South Poles of Earth will melt and add water to the oceans. And if the ice does melt, will it be a partial, slow trickle or a complete, sudden meltdown?

The following article examines the evidence of rising seas and melting polar ice, and our ability to predict what will happen next. The author suggests that as long as the sea rises slowly,

*chances are coastal communities will have
time to prepare and protect themselves.
However, if the sea rises suddenly, flooding
could be catastrophic. —KW*

"The Rising Seas"
by David Schneider
Scientific American, March 1997

Many people were awakened by the air-raid sirens.
Others heard church bells sounding. Some probably
sensed only a distant, predawn ringing and returned to
sleep. But before the end of that day—February 1,
1953—more than a million Dutch citizens would learn
for whom these bells tolled and why. In the middle of
the night, a deadly combination of winds and tides had
raised the level of the North Sea to the brim of the
Netherlands' protective dikes, and the ocean was
beginning to pour in.

As nearby Dutch villagers slept, water rushing over
the dikes began to eat away at these earthen bulwarks
from the back side. Soon the sea had breached the
perimeter, and water freely flooded the land, eventually
extending the sea inward as far as 64 kilometers from
the former coast. In all, more than 200,000 hectares of
farmland were inundated, some 2,000 people died, and
roughly 100,000 were left homeless. One sixth of the
Netherlands was covered in seawater.

With memories of that catastrophe still etched in
people's minds, it is no wonder that Dutch planners

took a keen interest when, a quarter century later, scientists began suggesting that global warming could cause the world's oceans to rise by several meters. Increases in sea level could be expected to come about for various reasons, all tied to the heating of the earth's surface, which most experts deem an inevitable consequence of the mounting abundance of carbon dioxide and other heat-trapping "greenhouse gases" in the air.

First off, greenhouse warming of the earth's atmosphere would eventually increase the temperature of the ocean, and seawater, like most other substances, expands when heated. That thermal expansion of the ocean might be sufficient to raise sea level by about 30 centimeters or more in the next 100 years.

A second cause for concern has already shown itself plainly in many of Europe's Alpine valleys. For the past century or two, mountain glaciers there have been shrinking, and the water released into streams and rivers has been adding to the sea. Such meltwaters from mountain glaciers may have boosted the ocean by as much as five centimeters in the past 100 years, and this continuing influx will most likely elevate sea level even more quickly in the future.

But it is a third threat that was the real worry to the Dutch and to the people of other low-lying countries. Some scientists began warning more than 20 years ago that global warming might cause a precariously placed store of frozen water in Antarctica to melt, leading to a calamitous rise in sea level—perhaps five or six meters' worth.

Yet predicting exactly how—or whether—sea level will shift in response to global warming remains a significant challenge. Scientists trained in many separate disciplines are attempting to glean answers using a variety of experimental approaches, ranging from drilling into the Antarctic ice cap to bouncing radar off the ocean from space. With such efforts, investigators have learned a great deal about how sea level has varied in the past and how it is currently changing. For example, most of these scientists agree that the ocean has been creeping upward by two millimeters a year for at least the past several decades. But determining whether a warmer climate will lead to a sudden acceleration in the rate of sea level rise remains an outstanding question.

Antarctic Uncertainties

One of the first prominent geologists to raise concern that global warming might trigger a catastrophic collapse of the Antarctic ice cap was J. H. Mercer of Ohio State University. Because the thick slab of ice covering much of West Antarctica rests on bedrock well below sea level, Mercer explained in his 1978 article "West Antarctic Ice Sheet and CO_2 Greenhouse Effect: A Threat of Disaster," this "marine ice sheet" is inherently unstable. If the greenhouse effect were to warm the south polar region by just five degrees Celsius, the floating ice shelves surrounding the West Antarctic ice sheet would begin to disappear. Robbed of these buttresses, this grounded ice sheet—a vestige of the last ice age—

would quickly disintegrate, flooding coastlines around the world in the process.

Mercer's disaster scenario was largely theoretical, but he pointed to some evidence that the West Antarctic ice sheet may, in fact, have melted at least once before. Between about 110,000 and 130,000 years ago, when the last shared ancestors of all humans probably fanned out of Africa into Asia and Europe, the earth experienced a climatic history strikingly similar to what has transpired in the past 20,000 years, warming abruptly from the chill of a great ice age.

That ancient warming may have achieved conditions that were a bit more balmy than at present. The geologic record of that time (known to the cognoscenti as inter-glacial stage 5e) remains somewhat murky, yet many geologists believe sea level stood about five meters higher than it does now—just the additional dollop that would be provided by the melting of the West Antarctic ice sheet. If such a collapse had occurred in Antarctica during a slightly hotter phase in the past, some reasoned, the current warming trend might portend a repeat performance.

That possibility spurred a group of American investigators to organize a coordinated research program in 1990, to which they attached the title "SeaRISE" (for Sea-level Response to Ice Sheet Evolution). The report of their first workshop noted some ominous signs on the southernmost continent, including the presence of five active "ice streams" drawing ice from the interior of West Antarctica into the nearby Ross

Sea. They stated that these channels in the West Antarctic ice sheet, where glacial ice flows rapidly toward the ocean, "may be manifestations of collapse already under way."

But more recent research suggests that the dire warnings expressed up to that time may have been exaggerated. In the early 1990s, researchers using so-called global circulation models, complex computer programs with which scientists attempt to predict future climate by calculating the behavior of the atmosphere and ocean, began investigating how a warmed climate would affect the Antarctic ice cap. These researchers found that greenhouse heating would cause warmer, wetter air to reach Antarctica, where it would deposit its moisture as snow. Even the sea ice surrounding the continent might expand.

In other words, just as SeaRISE scientists were beginning to mount their campaign to follow the presumed collapse of the West Antarctic ice sheet, computer models were showing that the great mass of ice in the Antarctic could grow, causing sea level to drop as water removed from the sea became locked up in continental ice. "That really knocked the wind out of their sails," quips Richard G. Fairbanks, a geologist at the Columbia University Lamont-Doherty Earth Observatory.

Other observations have also steered the opinion of many scientists working in Antarctica away from the notion that sudden melting there might push sea level upward several meters sometime in the foreseeable future. For example, glaciologists now realize that the five major ice streams feeding the Ross Sea (named, rather uninventively, ice streams A, B, C, D and E) are not all relentlessly disgorging their contents into the ocean. One of the largest, ice stream C, evidently stopped moving about 130 years ago, perhaps because it lost lubrication at its base.

In fact, the connection between climatic warming and the movement of West Antarctic ice streams has become increasingly tenuous. Ellen Mosley-Thompson of the Ohio State University Byrd Polar Research Center notes that ice streams "seem to start and stop, and nobody really knows why." And her own measurements of the rate of snow accumulation near the South Pole show that snowfalls have mounted substantially in recent decades, a period in which global temperature has inched up; observations at other sites in Antarctica have yielded similar results.

But the places in Antarctica being monitored in this way are few and far between, Mosley-Thompson emphasizes. Although many scientists are now willing to accept that human activities have contributed to global warming, no one can say with any assurance whether the Antarctic ice cap is growing or shrinking in response. "Anybody who tells you that they know is being dishonest," she warns.

That uncertainty could disappear in just a few years if the National Aeronautics and Space Administration is successful in its plans to launch a satellite designed to map changes in the elevation of the polar ice caps

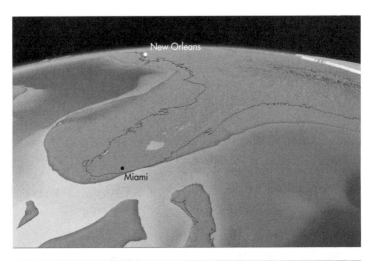

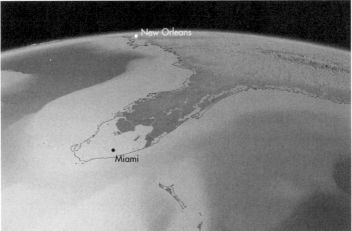

Florida looked quite different 20,000 years ago, during the last ice age. At that time, vast amounts of water remained locked within continental ice sheets to the north, and sea level was nearly 120 meters lower than today (*top*). As the ice melted, the coastlines retreated inland to their present positions (*black line*). Future melting of ice in West Antarctica may yet raise sea level an additional five meters, inundating large areas (*bottom*).

with extraordinary accuracy—perhaps to within a centimeter a year. A laser range finder on this forthcoming satellite, which is scheduled to be placed in a polar orbit in 2002, should be capable of detecting subtle changes in the overall volume of snow and ice stored at the poles. (Curiously, a similar laser instrument is now on its way to Mars and will be charting changes in the frozen polar ice caps on that planet well before scientists are able to perform the same feat for the earth.) During the first decade of the 21st century, then, scientists should finally learn whether the Antarctic ice cap as a whole is releasing water to the sea or storing water away in deep freeze.

Further insight into the stability of West Antarctica's vast marine ice sheet may come sooner, after scientists drill deeply into the ice perched between two of the ice streams. The researchers planning that project (who have replaced their former moniker SeaRISE with the less alarmist acronym WAIS—for West Antarctic ice sheet) hope to recover ice, if it indeed existed, dating from the exceptionally warm 5e interval of 120,000 years ago. Finding such a sample of long-frozen West Antarctic ice would, in Mosley-Thompson's words, "give you some confidence in its stability."

Until those projects are completed, however, scientists trying to understand sea level and predict changes for the next century can make only educated guesses about whether the polar ice caps are growing or shrinking. The experts of the Intergovernmental Panel on Climate Change, a body established in 1988 by the

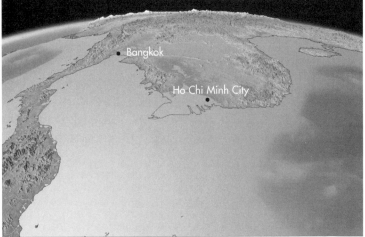

Southeast Asia during the last ice age included a huge tract of land along what is now the Sunda Shelf. That terrain connected the mainland of Asia with the islands of Indonesia, forming one great continental mass (*top*). Should the West Antarctic ice sheet melt, the resulting five-meter rise in sea level would flood river deltas, including the environs of Ho Chi Minh City and Bangkok (*bottom*), substantially altering the present coast (*black line*).

World Meteorological Organization and the United Nations Development Program, have adopted the position that both the Antarctic and the smaller Greenland ice caps are most likely to remain constant in size (although they admit the possibility of substantial errors in their estimate, acknowledging that they really do not know whether to expect growth or decay).

Up or Down?

Whatever the fate of the polar ice caps may be, most researchers agree that sea level is currently rising. But establishing that fact has been anything but easy. Although tide gauges in ports around the world have been measuring sea level for many decades, calculating the change in the overall height of the ocean is a surprisingly complicated affair. The essential difficulty is that land to which these gauges are attached can itself be moving up or down. Some regions, such as Scandinavia, are still springing back after being crushed by massive glaciers during the last ice age. Such postglacial rebound explains why sea level measured in Stockholm appears to be falling at about four millimeters a year, whereas it is rising by one and a half millimeters a year at Honolulu, a more stable spot.

In principle, one could determine the true rise in sea level by throwing out the results from tide gauges located where landmasses are shifting. But that strategy rapidly eliminates most of the available data. Nearly all the eastern seaboard of North America, for instance, is still settling from its formerly elevated position on a "peripheral bulge," a raised lip that surrounded the depression created by the great ice sheet that covered eastern Canada 20,000 years ago. What is more, local effects—such as the buckling that occurs at the edges of tectonic plates or the subsidence that ensues when water or oil is pumped from the ground—dominate in many tide gauge records, even in the tropics. In Bangkok, for instance, where residents have been tapping groundwater at a growing rate, subsidence makes it appear as if the sea has risen by almost a full meter in the past 30 years.

Fortunately, geophysicists have devised clever ways to overcome some of these problems. One method is to compute the motions expected from post-glacial rebound and subtract them from the tide gauge measurements. Using this approach, William R. Peltier and A. M. Tushingham, then both at the University of Toronto, found that global sea level has been rising at a rate of about two millimeters a year over the past few decades. Many other investigators, using different sets of records from tide gauges, have reached similar conclusions.

Further confirmation of this ongoing elevation of the ocean's surface comes from four years of measurements performed by the TOPEX/Poseidon satellite, which carries two radar altimeters aimed downward at the ocean. Because the position of the satellite in space is precisely known, the radar measurements of distance to the sea below can serve as a spaceborne tide gauge. The primary purpose of the TOPEX/Poseidon mission is to measure water circulation in the ocean by tracking surface undulations caused by currents. But the satellite has also been successful in discerning overall changes in the level of the ocean.

"When you average over the globe, you get much less variability than at an individual tide gauge," explains R. Steven Nerem of the Center for Space Research at the University of Texas at Austin. His published results from the TOPEX altimeter, which indicated that global sea level was rising at almost four millimeters a year—twice the rate previously determined—were, as it turns out, affected by a bug in the software used to process the satellite data. A subsequent analysis appears to confirm the land-based assessment of two millimeters a year in sea-level rise. "Of course, this estimate changes every time I put in some more data," Nerem admits, "but the current number is completely compatible with the estimates that have come from 50 years of tide gauge records."

Looking Backward

With few exceptions, scientists believe they have established a reliable value for the rate of recent rise in sea level: two millimeters a year. But the key question still facing these researchers—and civil planners—is whether this trend will hold steady or begin to accelerate in response to warming climate. Geologists have helped address this problem by tracing how sea level has fluctuated in the past, in response to prehistoric climate changes.

Columbia's Fairbanks, for example, has studied one species of coral that grows near the surface of the sea, particularly in and around the Caribbean. By drilling deeply into coral reefs in Barbados and locating ancient samples of this surface-dwelling species, he and his colleagues were able to follow the ascent of sea level since the end of the last ice age, when tremendous quantities of water were still trapped in polar ice caps and the oceans were about 120 meters lower than they are today.

Although his coral record shows episodes when the sea mounted by as much as two or three centimeters a year, Fairbanks notes that "these rates are for a very different world." At those times, 10,000 to 20,000 years ago, the great ice sheets that had blanketed much of North America and Europe were in the midst of melting, and the ocean was receiving huge influxes of water. The more recent part of the sea-level record indicates a progressive decline in the rate of ascent, with the height of the ocean seemingly stagnating in the past few millennia. Thus, the current climatological regime appears inclined toward relatively stable sea level.

But this reassuring picture is called into question by John B. Anderson, a marine geologist at Rice University. The data collected by Fairbanks and his colleagues are "not accurate enough to see the kinds of events predicted by the glaciological models," Anderson contends. There were at least three episodes of sudden sea-level rise in the past 10,000 years, he elaborates, but these are invisible in the coral record simply because "there's a five-meter error bar associated with that method."

Anderson and his co-workers have garnered evidence from such places as Galveston Bay in the Gulf of Mexico, where sediment cores and seismic soundings reveal how that estuary responded to rising sea level since the last ice age. A steady increase in sea level would have caused the underwater environments that characterize different parts of the estuary to move gradually landward. But the geologic record from Galveston Bay, Anderson says, shows "very dramatic" features that indicate sudden flooding of the ancient strand.

The most recent episode of sudden sea-level rise that Anderson discerns occurred about 2000 BC, when global climate was presumably similar to present conditions. His work indicates that sea level may have jumped considerably in just a few centuries. But so far Anderson has been unable to establish just how large a rise occurred.

Archaeologists should be able to help track ancient changes in sea level with further examination of coastal sites submerged by rising seas. Numerous analyses done so far in the Mediterranean, which span only the past 2,000 years, indicate that sea level has risen an average of only two tenths of a millimeter a year. Unfortunately, those studies give little insight into whether the ocean may have suddenly mounted 4,000 years ago. Nor is the archaeological work yet adequate to discern exactly when sea level began to quicken in its rise, ultimately reaching the modern rate of two millimeters a year.

Despite many such troubling gaps in the scientific understanding of how sea level has varied in the past and how it could change in the future, the experts of the Intergovernmental Panel on Climate Change have provided some broad guidelines for what the world might expect by the end of the next century. The panel's forecasts for sea-level rise range from 20 centimeters to almost one meter. The low end of these estimates corresponds, in essence, to the rate of sea-level rise that has probably been occurring for the past century or two—since before humanity began releasing carbon dioxide and other greenhouse gases into the atmosphere with abandon. That is to say, the next century might see only a continuation of the natural rise in sea level that has long been tolerated. The high-end estimate of the panel represents a substantial acceleration that could plausibly happen but so far has not been evidenced.

Weathering the Future

Of course, responsible international authorities must take the full range of possibilities into account in planning for the future. Although the fivefold uncertainty in the amount of sea-level rise might trouble some, John G. de Ronde, the head of hydraulic modeling at the Ministry of Transport and Public Works in the Netherlands, seems unruffled by it. Whatever the eventual trend in global sea level, he is confident that his country can cope: "Sea-level rise—you can measure that, you can see it and do something about it."

Although the necessary expenditures might seem enormous, de Ronde reports that the cost of improving Dutch dikes and other waterworks to accommodate 60 centimeters of sea-level rise over the next century amounts to no more than what people there now pay to maintain their bicycle paths. He shows greater concern for poor, land-scarce coastal nations and for an aspect of future climate that is much more difficult to forecast than sea level: changes in the frequency and intensity of violent storms. "You would need 20 years to see a change in statistics," de Ronde notes, "then a bad storm could happen the next day."

So as long as the West Antarctic ice sheet remains reasonably behaved, the real question facing residents of coastal regions may be how greenhouse warming affects local weather extremes and the size of damaging storm surges. Yet for those kinds of changes, scientists are especially hard put to offer predictions. Perhaps with further research and more refined computer models, climatologists will eventually be able to pinpoint where conditions will deteriorate and where they will improve. But such precise forecasts may, in the final reckoning, prove to be unreliable. It may just be as de Ronde says, imparting a lesson that nature keeps forcing on him and his colleagues: "We have to live with things we don't know exactly."

Changes in ocean temperature aren't easy to measure. You can't just stick a thermometer in every inch of seawater to take the temperature, so scientists have come up with more innovative methods. One way is to measure temperature using sound. Sound travels faster in warm water than in cold water. You can make a sound underwater and measure how long it takes to travel a certain distance; by analyzing thousands of measurements, you can determine the temperature of the water over huge areas.

This clean, accurate, and relatively inexpensive method created a new way for scientists to monitor the temperature of the oceans. The following article is about the scientist Walter H. Munk, who helped create and test the temperature technique that has become wildly popular, but also controversial, as some fear that the sound it generates is harmful to marine animals.

In recent years, the potentially harmful effects of sound on marine life has been gaining attention. Some research indicates that sound causes whales to become disoriented, for example, sometimes stranding themselves on beaches. Other research shows marine mammals abandoning good habitats to apparently get away from underwater noise. But the research is inconclusive. More than ten years after this article was first published, we still don't have clear answers. —KW

"The Man Who Would Hear Ocean Temperatures"
by Philip Yam
Scientific American, January 1995

Walter H. Munk is ripping off his necktie. "I had to give a talk earlier," he explains almost apologetically. Southern California casual appears to rule in Munk's office, where the sound of the surf and the smell of the sea relax even the most anxiety-ridden visitor from the Northeast.

Despite the surrounding calm, the spry 77-year-old Munk charges ahead in his tasks, as he has for more than half a century at the Scripps Institution of Oceanography in La Jolla, Calif. Gracious and quick to smile, he leads me on a tour midway through our interview, eager to show off his institute and the cable-stayed bridge that connects it to the newer parts of Scripps. He explains how he and his wife, Judith, an architect by training, helped to design the center, whose buildings are carved into the uneven slopes of the coastline.

Matters of the high seas, however, make Munk most comfortable. While I sip the coffee he has poured me, Munk checks his electronic mail. "We heard yesterday that the U.S. Navy is planning to close their listening station at Bermuda," he reports in his slightly Austrian accent. Dismantling the post—originally designed to locate Soviet submarines—would take place in less than two weeks, and Munk and his colleagues have sprung into action. "Our plan is to persuade the navy to give it to us," Munk comments. Scientists could then listen for undersea earthquakes and monitor the migration of marine mammals.

Munk's persistence is not surprising. Associates have described him—in a positive way—as a consummate salesman. His irresistible, infectious enthusiasm for what he does has won over many researchers and funding administrators. Indeed, Munk has been called one of the most influential oceanographers alive. "You say it in front of my wife tonight, and I know what she will say," Munk predicts. "Some four-letter word." (At dinner later, his wife resists, declaring she does not know me well enough.)

"What makes him a good scientist," remarks Carl Wunsch of the Massachusetts Institute of Technology and a longtime collaborator, "is his ability to see right through the math, to what it means physically." Munk's work has garnered him more than two dozen honors and awards, including the Vetlesen Prize, sometimes called the Nobel in earth science.

Nevertheless, Munk's stature received a bit of bruising recently. Environmental groups characterized his latest proposed experiment as deadly to marine mammals. To test climate models, Munk and his co-workers want to fire low-frequency sound waves off Kauai, Hawaii, and Point Sur, Calif. At a certain depth in the ocean, the temperature and pressure allow sound to travel thousands of kilometers without significant attenuation. Because sound moves faster in warm water than in cold water, changes in its average velocity can be measured over many years. The goal of the project, called acoustic thermometry of the ocean climate (ATOC), is to verify predictions by climate models that global warming is occurring. Legal maneuvers and political action have already delayed the project by more than two years. Opponents argue that the rumbles could harm whales by disrupting their communication or by deafening and possibly killing them. "Certainly, whales can hear for several tens of kilometers, and it might interfere with their mating and feeding habits," Munk acknowledges. "It's a legitimate concern."

But one that has been blown out of proportion, the oceanographer insists. "It started out because there was a mistake made," Munk says. A postdoctoral student had the units wrong. "We would be transmitting 250 watts acoustic," Munk explains. "You don't physically damage at 250 watts, just as I don't physically damage you by talking to you." It would sound like a very loud orchestra a few meters away. "You wouldn't like it," he assures me, but the volume would do no harm. The student thought the level would be 250 million watts, which would be fatal to any life nearby. A story in the *Los Angeles Times* set off the reaction that threatened ATOC.

The uproar caught the investigators off guard. "We've been working in the field for years without any problems," Munk points out. A dry run of ATOC in 1991 did not reveal any danger. Conducted off Heard Island near Antarctica in the southern Indian Ocean, the experiment blasted sound waves that were heard across the world, proving the feasibility of measuring ocean temperatures acoustically. Munk had arranged for marine biologists to monitor any effects on whales: "It was 1,000 times louder than what we want to do now, and we didn't cause any distress to the marine mammals." Munk also claims that other sources are far more disruptive. "We are about as loud as a tanker, and there are 1,000 tankers in the world. And tankers go 24 hours a day. As now proposed, we would be transmitting only 2 percent of the time, so we'd be very much less than a tanker."

Part of the trouble stems from language in the environmental impact statements, which declare that the experiment may "take" several hundred thousand mammals. In addition to death, the word meant any effect on behavior. "If you turn on your source and a whale changes its course by 10 degrees, you've taken him, by definition," Munk elaborates.

The controversy has abated, although at least one advocacy group remains, in Munk's words, "hostile." After obtaining the requisite permits, the ATOC workers hope to set sail this spring. "On the other hand, almost anyone can sue us," Munk observes. "You know, Scripps was concerned about the environment before the word 'environmentalist' had ever been used. To accuse the institution of being engaged in wholesale slaughter I think is terribly insulting."

Munk never anticipated that he would become an oceanographer. "I really grew up being interested only in skiing and tennis. Certainly not science," he states.

His Viennese upbringing centered around finance. His grandfather was a banker who left enough money to provide for his children as well as a thriving branch in New York City. So at age 14 Munk was shipped to U.S. shores. "I was supposed to follow him," he laments. "My mother was kind enough to say that if I gave it a real try for a couple of years and didn't want it, I could do whatever I wanted. I didn't like it all. Gee, I never liked banks—they're boring." Munk chuckles. "The only time banks are willing to lend you money is when you don't need it."

Driven by ennui, Munk decided to get as far away from New York as possible. "I read the brochures and fell in love with those wonderful California names like Pasadena, San Marino. And the pictures looked very romantic." He ended up on the steps of the California Institute of Technology. "I was terribly naive," Munk reminisces. "I hadn't applied. I just showed up and knocked on the dean's door. I thought that was all it took." Perhaps amazed at the naivete, the dean gave him an entrance examination, which Munk barely managed to pass.

Once enrolled, he studied applied physics, contemplating a career in geophysics. That notion quickly shifted. "I had a girlfriend whose grandparents were living in La Jolla, and she spent the summers there." Munk trailed her, taking a job at Scripps to pay for his living expenses. The woman dropped out of his life, but he liked Scripps so much that he returned to earn his doctorate under oceanographer Harald Sverdrup.

It was during World War II that Munk began a lifelong association with the navy. "I joined the army because I thought the end of the world was coming. Then the navy started some antisubmarine warfare," in which Roger Revelle, the late former director of Scripps, and Sverdrup were involved. They requested Munk be discharged from the army so that he could work alongside them. The switch was fortuitous. A few days later the Japanese attacked Pearl Harbor. "My unit had gone to New Guinea and was wiped out," Munk recalls. With Sverdrup, Munk predicted the occurrence of suitable waves that enabled Allied amphibious landings in northwestern Africa.

His military work constitutes only a small percentage of his contributions to earth science. "You'll see that I've been a dabbler," Munk remarks. "I do something for 10 years, then I do something else." With Scripps geophysicist Gordon J. MacDonald, he explained in the 1950s why the earth's axis wobbles and its spin varies slightly. In the 1960s he showed that storms near Antarctica give rise to the long, regular train of swells that rolls into southern California during the summer. In the 1970s he worked with Wunsch to develop ocean acoustic tomography. The technique, which relies on sound waves to create three-dimensional maps of ocean temperature and currents, led Munk directly to his present work on ocean climate.

"The inevitable outcome is that I don't do anything very well, because I don't stick with it long enough," Munk chides himself. "I'm not much of a scholar. I don't like to read. I like to work in a field that has nothing published, where you have to figure it out for yourself."

After dinner, Judith Munk leads the way to the deck to show me what they have chiseled into their backyard: an elegant amphitheater, large enough to accommodate 100 guests. Having been stricken with polio, she relies on a wheelchair for mobility. "We live very near to Jonas Salk," Walter mentions, "and we often accuse him if he hadn't been so damn lazy, if he had gotten his thing out a couple of years sooner, Judy wouldn't have come down with it." Munk laughs and throws up his hands: "He pleads guilty."

Although not a scientist, Judith has been instrumental in Walter's career—from taking the 4 AM ocean-swell watch in the Samoa Islands to influencing his thinking. "She has tremendously good common sense," Munk says. "She tells me when I do something stupid." Neither of the couple's two daughters is a scientist, although Walter likes to point out that one is married to a chemist.

On the deck, Judith encourages me to remove the drop cloth draped over the telescope that points out to sea. Only the light from a distant helicopter pierces the dark Pacific sky. By day the view of the ocean must be spectacular. "I love going to sea," Walter Munk muses. "It's a wonderful job."

Scientists are studying an ice sheet in West Antarctica that is about the size of Mexico. If it melts entirely, it has the potential to raise sea level by 5 to 6 meters (16 to 20 feet). Already, scientists have determined the glacier is shrinking by about 120 meters (394 ft) per day. The surprise is, it's been shrinking for thousands of years. This makes modern global warming an unlikely cause. Rather, the glacier is probably reacting to an ancient change in climate or ocean condition. We know that Earth's history has been naturally dotted with very cold and very warm periods, but in this case the scientific record complicates, rather than clarifies, our current understanding. The following article details the attempts of scientists to predict the fate of West Antarctica and what, if anything, can be done to stop its slow melt. —KW

"Melting Away"
by Sarah Simpson
Scientific American, January 2000

For years, scientists have feared that the earth's ever toastier climate could melt enough polar ice to swamp populated coastal areas such as New York City. Of greatest concern is West Antarctica, which by itself harbors enough water in its frozen clutches to raise sea level by the height of a two-story home.

Now new geologic evidence and one-of-a-kind satellite images are shedding light on West Antarctica's disappearing act. The bad news: the ice sheet may continue to shrink whether or not humanity curbs its release of heat-trapping greenhouse gases. The good news: its potential collapse may be slow enough that people will have time to move their cities out of harm's way.

Scientists worry about the West Antarctic ice sheet more than its counterparts in East Antarctica and Greenland, which cover bedrock that sits well above sea level. In contrast, West Antarctica's rocky foundation lies up to 2,500 meters below the ocean surface. The danger is that if the ice shelves that extend seaward from the continent start floating higher, they may pull the "grounded" ice away from the bedrock, making it more apt to crack into icebergs and melt. A complete breakup of the ice sheet, which is about the size of Mexico, would raise sea level by five or six meters.

For the first time, researchers have dated the retreat of the ice sheet's contact with the ground—a good way to determine how fast it is disappearing. Brenda L. Hall of the University of Maine and her colleagues knew from previous research that the ice sheet had extended 1,300 kilometers beyond its current position in the Ross Sea Embayment at the peak of the last ice age, 20,000 years ago.

As the planet warmed, the ice that had gripped much of North America melted, the oceans swelled and the grounded ice in West Antarctica pulled away from the bedrock in response. To find out just how fast this separation happened, Hall and her team needed to figure out the age of a beach that had formed along the ice sheet after its first known step inland. The bits of organic matter needed to perform radiocarbon dating are difficult to come by in the barren Antarctic landscape. Trowels and tweezers in hand, Hall and her team often hiked 30 kilometers a day, scouring the rocky soil for the mollusk shells and sealskin that prove that seasonal open water must have existed there in the past.

Radiocarbon dates for the shells found at the oldest beach, which today juts out into the Ross Sea near McMurdo Sound, indicate that the region was free of grounded ice by 7,600 years ago. And based on organic beach material and radar images of the subsurface ice at two points farther inland, the ice has been retreating at an average rate of 120 meters per year ever since.

While Hall's team plotted how fast the edge of the ice sheet has been shrinking, a different research group has found evidence of when the ice began its retreat— using rocks stranded along the flanks of Mount Waesche volcano, which sits in the middle of the ice sheet and records the highest elevation the ice ever reached. "We use the volcano like a dipstick," says Robert P. Ackert, Jr., of the Woods Hole Oceanographic Institution. Ackert and his colleagues looked at the accumulation of cosmic particles that first struck the rocks when they were left exposed on the volcano, as the ice began to thin. The time that has passed since the rocks' exposure indicates that the ice did not begin its retreat until 10,000 years ago—at least 3,000 years after the oceans began to rise.

These findings together suggest that the ice of West Antarctica is slow to react and can continue to change even long after an external trigger—in this case, rising sea level—has stopped. What's more, the ice sheet shows no signs of halting its inland march, Hall says. At its current pace, it will disappear in 7,000 years regardless of global warming. But that prediction is extrapolated from only four past positions of the ice sheet. "We don't have enough data to know whether it has retreated in jumps and spurts," Hall notes.

Jumps and spurts are especially hard to predict because of the way the continent sheds its icy load. Antarctica may be shrinking, but oddly enough, it is not melting, at least not directly. Meltwater pours off Greenland's icy veneer, but in much colder West Antarctica "streams" of swift-moving ice do the shedding. Snow falls in the interior, and the streams carry ice to the sea, where it breaks into icebergs.

Until now, no one knew what was happening at the streams' source, but researchers are a giant leap closer to understanding just how these ice streams work, thanks to new images made by a Canadian satellite called Radarsat. On two occasions during the fall of 1997, the satellite measured reflections of cloud-penetrating radar over much of the ice sheet's thick interior upstream from the Ross Ice Shelf. Using a technique called interferometry, Ian R. Joughin of the

Jet Propulsion Laboratory in Pasadena, Calif., and his co-workers mathematically compared the two sets of reflections to determine the speed and direction of the ice at each point.

"You don't see the picture until you connect all the dots," Joughin says. "That's what our image does." In times past, a single velocity measurement required that someone go to the spot and plant a stake with a Global Positioning System receiver in the ice, leave for a certain amount of time, then go back and see how far it had moved. In the barren chill of the Antarctic, that's no easy task. "The step forward is just remarkable," says glaciologist Richard B. Alley of Pennsylvania State University. "In the past we were really unclear about what the ice sheet looked like and how it changes."

Before Radarsat, some specialists had suspected a stable "lake" of accumulating snow might feed these swift streams, but it turns out that long tributaries nourish the streams from snowy regions deeper in the ice sheet's interior. "There's always more chance for instability when the ice flow extends so far inland," Joughin says. These tributaries flow at about 100 meters per year—roughly 10 times as fast as the ice sheet itself. At that pace there could be enough friction that the ice is actually melting along the bottom, he adds.

Alley points out that lubricated streambeds are probably not new. Ice has been sliding quickly out of the interior for a long time, he notes: "Otherwise the ice would have been much thicker at Mount Waesche."

The satellite images also revealed that tributaries are still feeding one stream that previous researchers had given up for dead when it dammed up 140 years ago. That means if global warming melts ice elsewhere, rising sea level could tear up the Ross Ice Shelf and break the dam, which would allow ice from inland to flow faster, Joughin says.

Alley cautions that scientists are still far from being able to predict the fate of West Antarctica. "We'd like tell to you whether it's going to fall in the ocean, but there's a lot of fundamental science we still just don't know," he says. This summer Alley and his colleagues will begin analyzing a kilometer-long ice core from West Antarctica that could reveal whether the ice sheet vanished in the warm times before the last ice age. If it did, that may give New Yorkers and the rest of the world more reason to be wary of a future meltdown.

Global warming (a possible cause of changing ocean temperatures) happens when too much carbon dioxide (CO_2) is added to the air. One way to combat the effects of global warming is to remove this extra CO_2 from the air. For this task, scientists are investigating the use of plants. Plants are excellent at absorbing CO_2. They take in CO_2 and release oxygen for us to breathe. Forests have long been recognized as CO_2

absorbers, or "sinks." Now the tiny plants that live
in the ocean, called phytoplankton, are getting
some attention.

The following article is about how marine
phytoplankton help absorb extra CO_2 out of the
atmosphere—making the ocean a valuable CO_2
sink. Fertilizing phytoplankton to help the plant
populations grow could increase the CO_2-absorbing
potential of the oceans. If it worked, reducing the
amount of CO_2 in the atmosphere could lessen
global warming and help keep ocean temperatures
from changing too much. The idea is still being
studied today. —KW

"The Ocean's Invisible Forest"
by Paul G. Falkowski
Scientific American, August 2002

Every drop of water in the top 100 meters of the ocean
contains thousands of free-floating, microscopic flora
called phytoplankton. These single-celled organisms—
including diatoms and other algae—inhabit three
quarters of the earth's surface, and yet they account
for less than 1 percent of the 600 billion metric tons of
carbon contained within its photosynthetic biomass.
But being small doesn't stop this virtually invisible
forest from making a bold mark on the planet's most
critical natural cycles.

Arguably one of the most consequential activities
of marine phytoplankton is their influence on climate.

Until recently, however, few researchers appreciated the degree to which these diminutive ocean dwellers can draw the greenhouse gas carbon dioxide (CO_2) out of the atmosphere and store it in the deep sea. New satellite observations and extensive oceanographic research projects are finally revealing how sensitive these organisms are to changes in global temperatures, ocean circulation and nutrient availability.

With this knowledge has come a temptation among certain researchers, entrepreneurs and policymakers to manipulate phytoplankton populations—by adding nutrients to the oceans—in an effort to mitigate global warming. A two-month experiment conducted early this year in the Southern Ocean confirmed that injecting surface waters with trace amounts of iron stimulates phytoplankton growth; however, the efficacy and prudence of widespread, commercial ocean-fertilization schemes are still hotly debated. Exploring how human activities can alter phytoplankton's impact on the planet's carbon cycle is crucial for predicting the long-term ecological side effects of such actions.

Seeing Green

Over time spans of decades to centuries, plants play a major role in pulling CO_2 out of the atmosphere. Such has been the case since about three billion years ago, when oxygenic, or oxygen-producing, photosynthesis evolved in cyanobacteria, the world's most abundant type of phytoplankton. Phytoplankton and all land-dwelling plants—which evolved from phytoplankton

Overview/*Climate Regulators*

- Rapid life cycles of marine phytoplankton transfer heat-trapping carbon dioxide (CO_2) from the atmosphere and upper ocean to the deep sea, where the gas remains sequestered until currents return it to the surface hundreds of years later.
- If all of the world's marine phytoplankton were to die today, the concentration of CO_2 in the atmosphere would rise by 200 parts per million—or 35 percent—in a matter of centuries.
- Adding certain nutrients to the ocean surface can dramatically enhance the growth of phytoplankton and thus their uptake of CO_2 via photosynthesis, but whether intentional fertilization increases CO_2 storage in the deep sea is still uncertain.
- Artificially enhancing phytoplankton growth will have inevitable but unpredictable consequences on natural marine ecosystems.

about 500 million years ago—use the energy in sunlight to split water molecules into atoms of hydrogen and oxygen. The oxygen is liberated as a waste product and makes possible all animal life on earth, including our own. The planet's cycle of carbon (and, to a large extent, its climate) depends on photosynthetic organisms using the hydrogen to help convert the inorganic carbon in CO_2 into organic matter—the sugars, amino acids and other biological molecules that make up their cells.

This conversion of CO_2 into organic matter, also known as primary production, has not always been easy to measure. Until about five years ago, most biologists were greatly underestimating the contribution of phytoplankton relative to that of land-dwelling plants. In the second half of the 20th century, biological oceanographers made thousands of individual measurements of phytoplankton productivity. But these data points were scattered so unevenly around the world that the coverage in any given month or year remained extremely small. Even with the help of mathematical models to fill in the gaps, estimates of total global productivity were unreliable.

That changed in 1997, when NASA launched the Sea Wide Field Sensor (SeaWiFS), the first satellite capable of observing the entire planet's phytoplankton populations every single week. The ability of satellites to see these organisms exploits the fact that oxygenic photosynthesis works only in the presence of chlorophyll *a*. This and other pigments absorb the blue and green wavelengths of sunlight, whereas water molecules scatter them. The more phytoplankton soaking up sunlight in a given area, the darker that part of the ocean looks to an observer in space. A simple satellite measurement of the ratio of blue-green light leaving the oceans is thus a way to quantify chlorophyll—and, by association, phytoplankton abundance.

The satellite images of chlorophyll, coupled with the thousands of productivity measurements, dramatically improved mathematical estimates of overall primary productivity in the oceans. Although various research groups differed in their analytical approaches, by 1998 they had all arrived at the same startling conclusion: every year phytoplankton incorporate approximately 45 billion to 50 billion metric tons of inorganic carbon into their cells—nearly double the amount cited in the most liberal of previous estimates.

That same year my colleagues Christopher B. Field and James T. Randerson of the Carnegie Institution of Washington and Michael J. Behrenfeld of Rutgers University and I decided to put this figure into a worldwide context by constructing the first satellite-based maps that compared primary production in the oceans with that on land. Earlier investigations had suggested that land plants assimilate as much as 100 billion metric tons of inorganic carbon a year. To the surprise of many ecologists, our satellite analysis revealed that they assimilate only about 52 billion metric tons. In other words, phytoplankton draw nearly as much CO_2 out of the atmosphere and oceans through photosynthesis as do trees, grasses and all other land plants combined.

Sinking out of Sight

Learning that phytoplankton were twice as productive as previously thought meant that biologists had to reconsider dead phytoplankton's ultimate fate, which strongly modifies the planet's cycle of carbon and CO_2 gas. Because phytoplankton direct virtually all the energy they harvest from the sun toward photosynthesis and reproduction, the entire marine population can replace itself every week. In contrast, land plants must invest copious energy to build wood, leaves and roots and take an average of 20 years to replace themselves. As phytoplankton cells divide— every six days on average—half the daughter cells die or are eaten by zooplankton, miniature animals that in turn provide food for shrimp, fish and larger carnivores.

The knowledge that the rapid life cycle of phytoplankton is the key to their ability to influence climate inspired an ongoing international research program called the Joint Global Ocean Flux Study (JGOFS). Beginning in 1988, JGOFS investigators began quantifying the oceanic carbon cycle, in which the organic matter in the dead phytoplankton cells and animals' fecal material sinks and is consumed by microbes that convert it back into inorganic nutrients, including CO_2. Much of this recycling happens in the sunlit layer of the ocean, where the CO_2 is instantly available to be photosynthesized or absorbed back into the atmosphere. (The entire volume of gases in the atmosphere is exchanged with those dissolved in the upper ocean every six years or so.)

Most influential to climate is the organic matter that sinks into the deep ocean before it decays. When released below about 200 meters, CO_2 stays put for much longer because the colder temperature—and higher density—of this water prevents it from mixing with the warmer waters above. Through this process, known as the biological pump, phytoplankton remove CO_2 from the surface waters and atmosphere and store it in the deep ocean. Last year Edward A. Laws of the University of Hawaii, three other JGOFS researchers and I reported that the material pumped into the deep sea amounts to between seven billion and eight billion metric tons, or 15 percent, of the carbon that phytoplankton assimilate every year.

Within a few hundred years almost all the nutrients released in the deep sea find their way via upwelling and other ocean currents back to sunlit surface waters, where they stimulate additional phytoplankton growth. This cycle keeps the biological pump at a natural equilibrium in which the concentration of CO_2 in the atmosphere is about 200 parts per million lower than it would be otherwise—a significant factor considering that today's CO_2 concentration is about 365 parts per million.

Over millions of years, however, the biological pump leaks slowly. About one half of 1 percent of the dead phytoplankton cells and fecal matter settles into seafloor sediments before it can be recycled in the upper ocean. Some of this carbon becomes incorporated into sedimentary rocks such as black shales, the largest reservoir of organic matter on earth. An even smaller fraction forms deposits of petroleum and natural gas. Indeed, these primary fuels of the industrial world are nothing more than the fossilized remains of phytoplankton.

The carbon in shales and other rocks returns to the atmosphere as CO_2 only after the host rocks plunge deep into the earth's interior when tectonic plates collide at subduction zones. There extreme heat and pressure melt the rocks and thus force out some of the CO_2 gas, which is eventually released by way of volcanic eruptions.

By burning fossil fuels, people are bringing buried carbon back into circulation about a million times faster than volcanoes do. Forests and phytoplankton cannot absorb CO_2 fast enough to keep pace with these increases, and atmospheric concentrations of this greenhouse gas have risen rapidly, thereby almost certainly contributing significantly to the global warming trend of the past 50 years.

As policymakers began looking in the early 1990s for ways to make up for this shortfall, they turned to the oceans, which have the potential to hold all the CO_2 emitted by the burning of fossil fuels. Several researchers and private corporations proposed that artificially accelerating the biological pump could take advantage of this extra storage capacity. Hypothetically, this enhancement could be achieved in two ways: add extra nutrients to the upper ocean or ensure that nutrients not fully consumed are used more efficiently. Either way, many speculated, more phytoplankton would grow and more dead cells would be available to carry carbon into the deep ocean.

Phytoplankton's Influence on the Global Carbon Cycle

The earth's carbon cycle can dramatically influence global climate, depending on the relative amounts of heat-trapping carbon dioxide (CO_2) that move into and out of the atmosphere and upper ocean, which exchange gases every six years or so. Plantlike organisms called phytoplankton play four critical roles in this cycle. These microscopic ocean dwellers annually incorporate about 50 billion metric tons of carbon into their cells during photosynthesis, which is often stimulated by iron via windblown dust (1). Phytoplankton also temporarily store CO_2 in the deep ocean via the biological pump: about 15 percent of the carbon they assimilate settles into the deep sea, where it is released as CO_2 as the dead cells decay (2). Over hundreds of years, upwelling currents transport the dissolved gas and other nutrients back to sunlit surface waters.

A tiny fraction of the dead cells avoids being recycled by becoming part of petroleum deposits or sedimentary rocks in the seafloor. Some of the rock-bound carbon escapes as CO_2 gas and reenters the atmosphere during volcanic eruptions after millions of years of subduction and metamorphism in the planet's interior (3). Burning of fossil fuels, in contrast, returns CO_2 to the atmosphere about a million times faster (4). Marine phytoplankton and terrestrial forests cannot naturally incorporate

CO_2 quickly enough to mitigate this increase; as a consequence, the global carbon cycle has fallen out of balance, warming the planet. Some people have considered correcting this disparity by fertilizing the oceans with dilute iron solutions to artificially enhance phytoplankton photosynthesis and the biological pump. —*P. G. F.*

Fixes and Limits

Until major discoveries over the past 10 years clarified the natural distribution of nutrients in the oceans, scientists knew little about which ocean fertilizers would work for phytoplankton. Of the two primary nutrients that all phytoplankton need—nitrogen and phosphorus—phosphorus was long thought to be the harder to come by. Essential for synthesis of nucleic acids, phosphorus occurs exclusively in phosphate minerals within continental rocks and thus enters the oceans only via freshwater runoff such as rivers. Nitrogen (N_2) is the most abundant gas in the earth's atmosphere and dissolves freely in seawater.

By the early 1980s, however, biological oceanographers had begun to realize that they were overestimating the rate at which nitrogen becomes available for use by living organisms. The vast majority of phytoplankton can use nitrogen to build proteins only after it is fixed—in other words, combined with hydrogen or oxygen atoms to form ammonium (NH_4^+), nitrite (NO_2^-) or nitrate (NO_3^-). The vast majority of nitrogen is fixed by small subsets of bacteria and cyanobacteria that convert N_2 to ammonium, which is released into seawater as the organisms die and decay.

Within the details of that chemical transformation lie the reasons why phytoplankton growth is almost always limited by the availability of nitrogen. To catalyze the reaction, both bacteria and cyanobacteria use nitrogenase, an enzyme that relies on another element, iron, to transfer electrons. In cyanobacteria, the primary energy source for nitrogen fixation is another process that requires a large investment of iron—the production of adenosine triphosphate (ATP). For these reasons, many oceanographers think that iron controls how much nitrogen these special organisms can fix.

In the mid-1980s the late John Martin, a chemist at the Moss Landing Marine Laboratories in California, hypothesized that the availability of iron is low enough in many ocean realms that phytoplankton production is severely restricted. Using extremely sensitive methods to measure the metal, he discovered that its concentration in the equatorial Pacific, the northeastern Pacific and the Southern Ocean is so low that phosphorus and nitrogen in these surface waters are never used up.

Martin's iron hypothesis was initially controversial, in part because previous ocean measurements, which turned out to be contaminated, had suggested that iron was plentiful. But Martin and his coworkers pointed out that practically the only way iron reaches the surface waters of the open ocean is via windblown dust. Consequently, in vast areas of the open ocean, far removed from land, the concentration of this critical element seldom exceeds 0.2 part per billion—a fiftieth to a hundredth the concentrations of phosphate or fixed inorganic nitrogen.

Historical evidence buried in layers of ice from Antarctica also supported Martin's hypothesis. The Vostok ice core, a record of the past 420,000 years of the earth's history, implied that during ice ages the amount of iron was much higher and the average size of the dust particles was significantly larger than during warmer times. These findings suggest that the continents were dry and wind speeds were high during glacial periods, thereby injecting more iron and dust into the atmosphere than during wetter interglacial times.

Martin and other investigators also noted that when dust was high, CO_2 was low, and vice versa. This correlation implied that increased delivery of iron to the oceans during peak glacial times stimulated both nitrogen fixation and phytoplankton's use of nutrients. The resulting rise in phytoplankton productivity could have enhanced the biological pump, thereby pulling more CO_2 out of the atmosphere.

The dramatic response of phytoplankton to changing glacial conditions took place over thousands of years, but Martin wanted to know whether smaller changes could make a difference in a matter of days. In 1993 Martin's colleagues conducted the world's first open-ocean manipulation experiment by adding iron directly to the equatorial Pacific. Their research ship carried tanks containing a few hundred kilograms of iron dissolved in dilute sulfuric acid and slowly released the solution as it traversed a 50-square-kilometer patch of ocean like a lawn mower. The outcome of this first experiment was promising but inconclusive, in part because the seafaring scientists were able to schedule only about a week to watch the phytoplankton react. When the same group repeated the experiment for four weeks in 1995, the results were clear: the additional iron dramatically increased phytoplankton photosynthesis, leading to a bloom of organisms that colored the waters green.

Since then, three independent groups, from New Zealand, Germany and the U.S., have demonstrated unequivocally that adding small amounts of iron to the Southern Ocean greatly stimulates phytoplankton productivity. The most extensive fertilization experiment to date took place during January and February of this year. The project, called the Southern Ocean Iron Experiment (SOFeX) and led by the Monterey Bay Aquarium Research Institute and the Moss Landing Marine Laboratories, involved three ships and 76 scientists, including four of my colleagues from Rutgers. Preliminary results indicate that one ton of iron solution released over about 300 square kilometers resulted in a 10-fold increase in primary productivity in eight weeks' time.

These results have convinced most biologists that iron indeed stimulates phytoplankton growth at high latitudes, but it is important to note that no one has yet proved whether this increased productivity enhanced the biological pump or increased CO_2 storage in the deep sea. The most up-to-date mathematical predictions suggest that even if phytoplankton incorporated all the unused nitrogen and phosphorus in the surface waters of the Southern Ocean over the next 100 years, at most 15 percent of the CO_2 released during fossil-fuel combustion could be sequestered.

Fertilizing the Ocean

Despite the myriad uncertainties about purposefully fertilizing the oceans, some groups from both the private and public sectors have taken steps toward doing so on much larger scales. One company has proposed a scheme in which commercial ships that routinely traverse the southern Pacific would release small amounts of a fertilizer mix. Other groups have discussed the possibility of piping nutrients, including iron and ammonia, directly into coastal waters to trigger phytoplankton blooms. Three American entrepreneurs have even convinced the U.S. Patent and Trademark Office to issue seven patents for commercial ocean-fertilization technologies, and yet another is pending.

It is still unclear whether such ocean-fertilization strategies will ever be technically feasible. To be effective, fertilization would have to be conducted year in and year out for decades. Because ocean circulation will eventually expose all deep waters to the atmosphere, all the extra CO_2 stored by the enhanced biological pump would return to the atmosphere within a few hundreds years of the last fertilizer treatment. Moreover, the reach of such efforts is not easily controlled. Farmers cannot keep nutrients contained to a plot of land; fertilizing a patch of turbulent ocean water is even less manageable. For this reason, many ocean experts argue that that once initiated, large-scale fertilization could produce long-term damage that would be difficult, if not impossible, to fix.

Major disruptions to the marine food web are a foremost concern. Computer simulations and studies of natural phytoplankton blooms indicate that enhancing primary productivity could lead to local problems of severe oxygen depletion. The microbes that consume dead phytoplankton cells as they sink toward the seafloor sometimes consume oxygen faster than ocean circulation can replenish it. Creatures that cannot escape to more oxygen-rich waters will suffocate.

Such conditions also encourage the growth of microbes that produce methane and nitrous oxide, two greenhouse gases with even greater heat-trapping capacity than CO_2. According to the National Oceanic and Atmospheric Administration, severe oxygen depletion and other problems triggered by nutrient runoff have already degraded more than half the coastal waters in the U.S., such as the infamous "dead zone" in the northern Gulf of Mexico. Dozens of other regions around the world are battling similar difficulties.

Even if the possible unintended consequences of fertilization were deemed tolerable, any such efforts must also compensate for the way plants and oceans would respond to a warmer world. Comparing satellite observations of phytoplankton abundance from the early 1980s with those from the 1990s suggests that the ocean is getting a little bit greener, but several investigators have noted that higher productivity does not guarantee that more carbon will be stored in the deep ocean. Indeed, the opposite may be true. Computer simulations of the oceans and the atmosphere have shown that additional warming will increase stratification of the ocean as freshwater from melting glaciers and sea ice floats above denser, salty seawater. Such stratification would actually slow the biological pump's ability to transport carbon from the sea surface to the deep ocean.

New satellite sensors are now watching phytoplankton populations on a daily basis, and future small-scale fertilization experiments will be critical to better understanding phytoplankton behavior. The idea of designing large, commercial ocean-fertilization projects to alter climate, however, is still under serious debate among the scientific community and policymakers alike. In the minds of many scientists, the potential temporary human benefit of commercial fertilization projects is not worth the inevitable but unpredictable consequences of altering natural marine ecosystems. In any case, it seems ironic that society would call on modern phytoplankton to help solve a problem created in part by the burning of their fossilized ancestors.

The Author

Paul G. Falkowski is professor in the Institute of Marine and Coastal Sciences and the department of geology at Rutgers University. Born and raised in New York City, Falkowski earned his Ph.D. from the University of British Columbia in 1975. After completing a postdoctoral fellowship at the University of Rhode Island, he joined Brookhaven National Laboratory in 1976 as a scientist in the newly formed oceanographic sciences division. In 1997 he and Zbigniew Kolber of Rutgers University co-invented a specialized fluorometer that can measure phytoplankton productivity in real time. The next year Falkowski joined the faculty at Rutgers, where his research focuses on the coevolution of biological and physical systems.

4 Ocean Case Studies

The Gulf of Mexico is a case study in natural oil spills. Cracks deep in the floor of the gulf naturally seep oil—the same oil humans drill for and pump to use for fuel. But instead of being catastrophic for ocean life like sudden, accidental spills from oil tankers on the ocean surface, these natural oil seeps appear to support their own unique ecosystems. Giant tube worms, mussels, and deep-sea crabs reside near such seeps. Because there are few food sources on the deep seafloor, these animals have evolved to get energy from the oil and depend on it to live.

For companies drilling for deep-sea oil, this creates an interesting question: could drillers deplete all the oil, and thus the energy, from these ecosystems? If this were possible, such deep-sea ecosystems could quickly become endangered.

The following article suggests it's unlikely that any deep-sea communities in the Gulf of Mexico are starving due to nearby oil drilling— but you can bet scientists are watching. —KW

"Down and Out in the Gulf of Mexico"
by David Schneider
Scientific American, April 1995

People have long criticized oil companies for the accidental release of oil into the sea, but over the past decade a strange wrinkle has developed in the banner of environmental protection. Some scientists have begun to wonder whether drilling in the Gulf of Mexico could threaten marine life by, strangely enough, reducing oil leaks.

This curious twist results from two separate advances. Oil and gas developers have been moving drilling operations farther offshore, enticed by immense oil and gas fields previously thought to lie in water too deep to be economically tapped. At the same time, researchers have been uncovering unexpected richness and diversity in deep-dwelling marine life.

The work of both these groups has recently been focused on the Gulf floor's many natural oil seeps. Although sensitive instruments are sometimes needed to detect their subtle chemical traces, ambient effusions in the Gulf can be so great that they leave markings on the surface. Researchers have even discovered that some of these slicks are visible from space.

Most leaks, however, are hard to find. In the mid-1980s oil companies hired scientists from Texas A&M University to survey native petroleum seeps on the continental slope. The researchers stumbled on a surprisingly plentiful biota—fields of huge tube worms, giant mussels and deep-sea crabs. These groupings resemble the dense seafloor communities found several years earlier during exploration of the hydrothermal vents that form at sites of submarine volcanism where tectonic plates separate.

Like vent assemblages, petroleum-seep communities are isolated from sunlight, and their discoverers quickly realized that life there must rely on a food chain that begins with energy from the constant petrochemical bath. Bacteria living within the gill cells of the giant mussels, for example, provide for their hosts by metabolizing methane.

Soon after their discovery, protection of seep dwellers became a priority. "Initially we worried they would be so rare that we might have an endangered-species situation," remarks Ken Graham of the Minerals Management Service, the agency regulating oil and gas development in the Gulf. Because such development involves erecting platforms, setting huge anchors and laying vast stretches of undersea pipeline, the Minerals Management Service issued special guidelines in 1989 for work that might impinge on chemosynthetic fauna.

But continuing study revealed that seep organisms are not rare after all. Chemosynthetic communities seem to develop wherever substantial leaks occur on the deep seafloor, and there is little fear now that off-shore drilling could accidentally destroy some unique species. But could extraction of petroleum offshore reduce pressure to nearby seeps, thereby robbing these deep-sea enclaves of their basic foodstuffs?

Although somewhat far-fetched, the question is not completely academic. Graham reports that Texas wildcatters often found that the extraction of oil on land could cause nearby seeps to dry; there might be similar results offshore. Ian R. MacDonald of Texas A&M believes degradation of a seep by exploitation of its source reservoir is indeed possible, but "it has to be considered on a case-by-case basis."

Conoco, for instance, has a platform sited close to one of the most extensive chemosynthetic communities found so far in the Gulf, a place known as Bush Hill. "They are producing oil a mile away from it," MacDonald remarks, "but they believe they are not tapping the reservoir" used by the organisms. Geologists at Shell, a company active in exploiting deepwater fields, also feel confident that the reservoirs being drilled in the Gulf are not directly connected to any seafloor seeps.

So it would seem, for the time being at least, that the giant mussels and giant tubeworms as well as the giant corporations can continue to feed together happily in the Gulf.

When the oil tanker Exxon Valdez *crashed into a reef in Prince William Sound, Alaska, in 1989, thousands of miles of coastline were coated with oil, killing countless birds and mammals. Scientific*

studies to measure the health of the ecosystem as
it recovered were plentiful but inconsistent. Exxon,
the company responsible for the spill, deployed
scientists that concluded the area had recovered
by 1991. Other scientists found the Exxon results
difficult to accept and cited poor science. As
disagreement brewed and years passed, scientists began to realize that cleaning oil from the
sound may have done more harm than good.

This article examines the science of the spill
cleanup and recovery seven years after the
event. Today, almost two decades have passed
since the Valdez spill and the ecosystem is still
being studied. What scientists learn about
recovery and cleanup at Prince William Sound
could be good for the oceans in the long run
because, unfortunately, this is likely not the last
oil spill of its kind. —KW

"Sounding Out Science"
by Marguerite Holloway
Scientific American, October 1996

Standing in front of his favorite boulder, Alan J. Mearns
of the National Oceanic and Atmospheric Administration
holds aloft a series of pictures, comparing this year's
scene with those of the previous six. The rock is
certainly a nice one—potato-shaped as it is and covered
with a fuzz of light-brown *Fucus*, or rockweed—but that
alone cannot explain the photographic frenzy it triggers.

Mearns takes another shot of the rock, capturing in the frame his colleague Gary Shigenaka, who is taking a video of the same outcropping, as well as Dennis C. Lees, who is studying the beach adjacent to the rock. Meanwhile, as a fourth scientist quips about the Heisenberg uncertainty principle and clamors to get a picture of Mearns taking a picture of Shigenaka taking a picture of Lees and the rock, a photojournalist records the whole assemblage.

This concept of an image inside an image and so on to infinity, what the French call *mis-en-abîme*, provides one of the keys to understanding what has happened in Prince William Sound, Alaska, since the *Exxon Valdez* crashed into Bligh Reef in 1989. More important, it sheds light on how to interpret "recovery," a term that in the Sound means very different things to different people. The tanker spilled about 37,000 metric tons of North Slope oil, coating a total of 1,750 kilometers of shoreline and killing thousands of birds and animals. The accident was followed by massive infusions of money, lawyers and scientific studies into the same wilderness—and these inputs were about as clarifying as the coat of thick black crude itself.

For years, lawyers watched scientists watching other scientists watching an ecosystem that is little understood and infinitely variable; everyone used a different-size frame to peer through. The state of Alaska, the people who live on the Sound and the area's fishermen all wanted to document not only the extent of the devastation but the endurance of the spill's deleterious effects. Exxon wished to show the effectiveness of its intensive cleanup as well as the evanescent quality of the oil, which is, after all, a natural substance.

Exxon lost, both in court and out. In addition to $2.5 billion spent on cleanup, on claims and on reimbursing agencies for response expenses, the company is paying $900 million to the Trustees—a panel of state and federal agency representatives—for "restoration," another ill-defined term that has come to include buying land so as to protect it. This 1991 out-of-court settlement includes a reopener provision: if, between the years 2002 and 2006, other impacts of the oil spill come to light, the Trustees get $100 million more. Exxon, which is also due to pay $39.6 million to the region's fishermen and to Sound residents, plans to appeal a $5-billion punitive settlement.

The studies that Exxon and the state of Alaska—including the departments of Fish and Game and of Environmental Conservation—conducted to prove their respective points were kept largely secret until legal settlements were reached. This secrecy reduced most of the pillars of science to rubble: out went scientific dialogue, data sharing and, for some parties, peer review. Millions of dollars were shelled out in duplicate studies—that reached opposite conclusions. In a scathing review of post-spill research in this year's *Annual Review of Ecology and Systematics*, marine biologist Robert T. Paine and his colleagues at the University of Washington quote a juror grappling with these apparent paradoxes. Originally cited in the *American Lawyer*, the juror at the $5-billion punitive trial summed up many observers' feelings about the science: "You got a guy with four Ph.D.'s saying no fish were hurt, then you got a guy with four Ph.D.'s saying, yeah, a lot of fish were hurt. . . . They just kind of delete each other out."

Viewfinders

Now, seven years after the disaster, one can see the *mis-en-abîme* effect—or perhaps instead, the Sound uncertainty principle—at work. Scientists are still sparring, lawyers are still lurking around the edges of disputes, and both claim to be searching for the truth. Nevertheless, it is becoming obvious that, with a few exceptions, most of the frames people have been looking through as they study the Sound are too small to permit clear conclusions about the effects of the oil—suggesting that the next big spill may be a scientific fiasco as well. Further, it appears oil may not be the whole story: there may be much larger factors at play in the Sound.

Some of this perspective has become possible because Exxon recently published its studies in a thick blue volume, and the Trustees' tome came out this summer. Not surprisingly, almost every abstract in the Exxon book has the same refrain: by 1991 the Sound was well. To the oil company, recovery was defined as the reestablishment of a "healthy" biological community characteristic of the area. By this standard, even a biological community that was quite different from the one before the spill could, obviously, qualify as healthy.

If one scrutinizes Exxon's research, one can see how the company reached its conclusions. For example—and this will relate later to Mearns's favorite rock, still sitting at the beginning of this article but not forgotten there—the intertidal zone can appear very healthy, two years after the spill. This zone is usually one of the most biologically active and important in marine ecosystems. *Fucus* and other algae anchor to tidally flooded rocks there; barnacles, drills, periwinkles, mussels, sea anemones, starfish, sea urchins, baby herring, pink salmon eggs, tiny sculpins, hermit crabs and other creatures that are part of the immense food web thrive in this rich, diverse place. Ravenous sea otters rake the intertidal, as do oyster-catchers and Harlequin ducks, searching for mussels and other invertebrates.

Looking through tiny frames called quadrats, Exxon contractor Edward S. Gilfillan of Bowdoin College and his team saw something quite different from what other intertidal researchers saw. Biologists lay down a quadrat on the spot they want to investigate and count every organism inside the boundaries. They then repeat this procedure many times, comparing species composition and diversity between beaches—in this case, oiled beaches versus unoiled ones. Frames can also be placed at different elevations—the lower, the middle and the upper intertidal—or along "transects" perpendicular to the water. In places such as Prince William Sound, the intertidal is normally patchy and uneven, so that within a foot of a *Fucus*-matted rock, there may be a naked boulder; six inches to the right, there may be more *Fucus* and a bevy of barnacles.

At each of his sites, Gilfillan put down one baby quadrat, 12.5 by 25 centimeters, at four places along three transects. If he got, say, *Fucus* in one, none in the next and partial covering in the third, the beach looked extremely variable. And what he concluded, in essence, was that there was so much variability on any beach, it was almost impossible to distinguish oiled from unoiled sites: every beach resembled every other. Therefore, recovery had occurred.

The Importance of Being Random

Further, because his many sites had been chosen randomly—the cornerstone of all good field biology— Gilfillan's results could be extrapolated to the entire region. "By 1990 between 73 and 91 percent of the area had recovered," Gilfillan notes, adding that people mistakenly describe the Sound as a fragile ecosystem. "As anyone who has been through an Alaskan winter knows, it is not fragile. The animals and plants there are very good at making good their losses."

Needless to say, Gilfillan's findings bemuse some observers—among them, Charles H. Peterson, a marine scientist at the University of North Carolina at Chapel Hill. Peterson, who was an expert witness in various Sound-related trials, points out that the Exxon approach not only exploits the Sound's patchiness, it mixes species together, wreaking havoc with biodiversity. For example, Gilfillan lumps different kinds of barnacles together in measuring total barnacle cover. And to him, the barnacle cover in 1990 looked much the same at oiled and unoiled beaches. In truth, Peterson explains, the lumping was misleading: the oiled sites principally contained one kind of barnacle—a little opportunistic gray species called *Chthamalus dalli*—whereas the unoiled beaches had larger, more diverse barnacles.

In another grouping, Exxon counted worms in the lower intertidal and mixed these figures into totals for the number of organisms. Yet, Peterson cautions, those worms congregate at oily sites. It is akin to saying you have 100 creatures at place A and 100 at place B; therefore, place A and B are equivalent. In fact, 99 of the animals in place A could be worms that love to eat the microorganisms that love to eat oil. "I have never seen a data set in my life that combines these communities," Peterson exclaims. "Some have argued that what Exxon did was create a study that was inconclusive by design."

Whatever the study was designed to do, its results gave Exxon evidence that all was well in 1991, so the company stopped monitoring the intertidal in quantitative ways. (Exxon researchers continue to conduct counts of sea otters and birds.) The Trustees, for their part—with Exxon's fiscal contribution—are still watching, waiting for the long-term negative effects they are sure will manifest themselves.

Ernie Piper of the Alaska Department of Environmental Conservation, normally loquacious, hesitates for a long time before answering a question about recovery. "In terms of the ecology, that, in many ways, it appears to me, is a lot more resilient than we deserved," he says slowly. "At the same time, there are lots of effects from the spill and the cleanup that are not going to go away."

"I think it is an improved picture," adds Robert B. Spies of Applied Marine Sciences in Livermore, Calif., and the chief scientist for the Trustees panel. "But it is still variable, depending on what resource you are talking about. Pink salmon have improved, yet we are worried about the herring." The Trustees also remain concerned about sea otter populations and the intertidal.

The state's principal study of the intertidal, directed by Raymond C. Highsmith of the University of Alaska-Fairbanks, resembled Exxon's in that it used randomly selected sites. It differed in that it incorporated more transects at each site and more spacious quadrats (40 by 50 centimeters). Highsmith and his colleagues—among them, Michael S. Stekoll of the University of Alaska-Fairbanks—found a counterpoint to Gilfillan. By 1991 they saw only incomplete recovery.

And there the study stopped. Despite all the money available, the Trustees deemed the work too costly at its original price: $10 million for three additional years. Even when the biologists proposed doing half the sites one year, half the next, it was still not cheap enough: "There is a lot of politics," Stekoll says, explaining that the Trustees are under great pressure to use the $900 million to acquire land for the state, thereby protecting it from deforestation. Two hundred million dollars have already been spent to do so, and there are plans to spend about $180 million more.

As unfinished business, nonetheless, the study permits the Trustees to defer conclusions about recovery. "I would like to bring closure to this intertidal thing. It is a question of priorities," Spies notes.

The Way We Were

For the Trustees, "recovery" will occur when the Sound looks as it would have if the spill had not occurred. The biggest problem with this criterion is that no one really knows exactly what the Sound was like before the blanket of oil and scientists descended on it or how it would have evolved. The scientists have had to grapple with the absence of baseline data, except for a few specific species, including murres on the Barren Islands, killer whales, sea lions and, of course, the commercially crucial salmon.

To a lay traveler visiting Prince William Sound this summer for the first time since 1991, it appears beautiful and healthy. Although oil still lies under the boulders and cobbles on some beaches, it takes longer to find, and the oil is largely weathered—that is, non-toxic. Humpback whales can be seen in open water before they dive, flashing their *Fucus*- or barnacle-encrusted tails. Also visible are orcas, porpoises, seals, sea lions, puffins, kittiwakes, pigeon guillemots and river otters in coves or channels. In one unoiled eastern bay, sea otters float everywhere, bobbing like buoys, some with young on their chests, while myriad bald eagles make their high-pitched, halting cries. And the intertidal, even in places that were heavily damaged, seems more luxuriant than it did five years ago—with purple and orange sea stars and tousled green, brown and red seaweed.

This big picture, however, can be just as misleading as a little quadrat. And that is why Mearns's rock is so interesting. Mearns belongs to yet another intertidal team, funded by NOAA. The NOAA study was designed differently from those of Exxon and the state, because it was never intended to be part of damage assessment— that is, it was not driven by litigation. Instead its agenda was to describe differences in recovery between oiled beaches that were left alone and those that were cleaned with high-pressure jets of very hot water.

Given that they spend most of their time on the beach staring into fairly big quadrats—50 by 50 centimeters—it is perhaps not surprising that Mearns and the rest of the NOAA team constantly joke about views and frames. Through these windows, this group— led by Jonathan P. Houghton of Pentec Environmental in Edmonds, Wash., and Lees of Ogden Environmental and Energy Services in San Diego—has watched recovery at many sites for the past seven years. Generally, they say, the intertidal looks good, although wide swings in species diversity and density persist.

The NOAA results suggest that hot-water cleaning sterilized the beaches; whatever survived the oiling did not survive the cure. The scientists report that a few years after the spill, the uncleaned beaches showed more health than did stark, cleaned sites. The finding—something oil spill experts warned about to no avail during the invasion of the cleanup crews—is not popular. Both Exxon and the state were, and are, under considerable public pressure to rid the Sound of every last inch of black veneer.

"Yeah, cleanup is disruptive, and if you clean up it is going to look like a very different shoreline," comments Piper of the Department of Environmental Conservation. But, he argues, as do some members of the NOAA team, hot-water washing just needs to be done more judiciously. One possible solution, Mearns suggests, is washing in strips, which would leave patches of beach oiled but alive so they can recolonize the bald spots.

The NOAA intertidal work has also been criticized on statistical grounds. Gilfillan of Exxon argues that because the sites were not randomly chosen, they have little statistical power and therefore are not generalizable. (According to a recent paper by Gilfillan, in which he and three colleagues compare the three intertidal studies, the Exxon study was statistically the most powerful.) Stekoll concurs: "From a pure statistical viewpoint, you would have to say that it was not a design to extrapolate to the Sound."

Houghton and Lees retort that they have fully characterized the biology of recovery—even if their sites were selected by different criteria, such as accessibility and the availability of baseline information (sometimes frantically gathered just before the oil came ashore). Thus, they are permitted to describe what is happening throughout the area. Statistics aside, it is true that by virtue of having monitored consistently for seven years, the NOAA crew has tracked some fascinating shifts in the ecosystem. And this is where the shaggy rock enters the picture again.

Mearns's subject sits in Snug Harbor, one of the loveliest places in the Sound. High mountains rise directly up from the shore, and a waterfall flows right onto the beach. Snug was heavily oiled and a large part of it left uncleaned, as "set-aside." Such places serve as important controls, allowing scientists to study how long it takes for oil to disappear naturally from various types of beaches. Nevertheless, set-asides are controversial: because most Alaskans wanted all oil removed, NOAA officials had to fight to get the few they have.

As a protected area, not scoured by winter waves, Snug is a particularly important reference. The harbor looks oil free these days, except for a small patch of asphalt, and the intertidal seems lush. But Mearns's photographs reveal that his Snug rock is going through a dramatic cycle. In 1990 its top was covered with young *Fucus*; in 1991 the rest of the rock sported a similar ensemble. Rockweed—a keystone of the intertidal ecosystem—was rebounding.

Or was it? If the NOAA workers had stopped there, they could have shared the stand with Gilfillan: the Sound looked recovered. But they went back, and in 1992 the rock had lost a lot of cover. The next year some scattered germlings covered the crown again; in 1994 it was naked; the cycle began anew in 1995. And this past summer Mearns found a fuller shag and a few small mussels in the crevices.

Mystery of the Vanishing Fucus

The NOAA scientists have seen this pattern in cleaned places as well. The hypothesis they present is that most intertidal zones contain *Fucus* plants of different ages, whereas in the oiled and the cleaned sites, most, if not all, of the *Fucus* was killed in 1989. The slate wiped clean, every subsequent plant that recolonized the site was the same age, with the same life span. So when the *Fucus* dies, taking most of the creatures it protects with it, the system returns to ground zero. This suggestion is bolstered by recent research on the coast of Britain, where the *Torrey Canyon* tanker spilled 119,000 tons of oil in 1967. *Fucus* there, it seems, still goes through similar cycles. "Ten years after *Torrey Canyon* they said it was fine," Lees states. "Now they are going back and seeing flux still." In particular, *Fucus* and limpets seem to be in a race for space.

There are anecdotal reports, however, that such die-offs are being seen in other, unoiled environments. And despite observations in the Sound, biologists admit that they do not really know all that much about the omnipresent algae. As Jennifer L. Ruesink of the University of Washington remarks, scientists are not even sure how to measure the age of *Fucus*. Is it necessarily older when it is darker? Does the number of dichotomies, or branches off a stem, reflect its age in years, like tree rings? How do adults help or hinder the establishment of young plants?

Ruesink tried to answer some of these questions as she accompanied the NOAA crew through the Sound over the summer; she sat on top of the Snug rock as well as many others, meticulously counting strands of *Fucus*, plying them apart. Her preliminary findings are "equivocal." It looks as though *Fucus* may have slip-slided away, even at sites never touched by oil. So the mystery remains.

The *Fucus* provides yet another frame through which to view the *Exxon Valdez* disaster. The basic questions asked about this seaweed give the real story away: nobody actually knows much about anything in the Sound—or in any such complicated ecosystem, for that matter. Most of the studies conducted in the early years after the spill centered on one zone, or one species, at a time.

But, as David Duffy of the University of Alaska-Anchorage puts it, you have a problem if your species—say, the otter—starts eating your colleague's, the mussel. It is more appropriate instead to try to examine from the outset how the frames fit within one another—like zooplankton inside herring inside salmon inside bear. Indeed, the relation between links in the food chain is proving to be perhaps the most important information that could be gleaned from science in the Sound.

A Bird's-Eye View

The opportunity for real insight may, however, have been squandered. "The tragedy is that people are trying to look at oil spill relations seven years after the fact," Duffy explains. "There should have been greater thinking about an ecosystem approach." Spies of the Trustees agrees: "We are very aware that looking on a species-by-species basis has limitations. We thought that that was very appropriate at the time of the spill to learn what was killed." Still, he notes, "we have got some very exciting projects right now that go beyond 'When did this resource recover?' to the basic processes going on in the ecosystem." The panel is funding several studies that take this wider perspective, looking at oceanographic trends in the Gulf of Alaska and at the food web. The frame is hundreds of kilometers a side.

For his part, Duffy is looking at birds, evaluating declines reported among kittiwakes and pigeon guillemots. "We don't know whether it is the spill, or the spill and environmental change, or just environmental change," Duffy says. "We have victims, we have the weapon, we have the [birds] at the scene of the crime, but we don't know whether something happened before that affected the population and that this spill was only the trigger. And we will never know."

What Duffy and others are piecing together is that the Gulf of Alaska, and Prince William Sound with it, seems to be going through a shift that predates the spill. Researchers have already had trouble teasing apart the pre-spill effects of an extremely cold winter in 1989; those of a 9.2-magnitude earthquake in 1964 that upturned the Sound, devastating the ecosystem and wiping out communities of people; and those of the 1982–1983 El Niño (a periodic oceanic disturbance that affects weather and ocean currents).

According to the only long-term study of bait fish in the region, the population of fatty pelagic fish on which sea lions, seals and many seabirds feed plummeted in the early 1980s. Today there are only 17 percent as many sea lions as there were 20 years ago. The shrimp fishery, which peaked at about 119 million pounds in 1976, was down to 10 million in 1982. "At that time, there was a lot of arrow slinging about overfishing," remarks Robert Otto of the National Marine Fisheries Service. "But the fact of the matter was that [shrimp] were declining both where they were fishing and where they were not."

Shrimp was the center of attention because it supports a large industry. But the problem did not stop there. Paul J. Anderson, also at the National Marine Fisheries Service, started sampling in the 1970s with a small mesh net and caught bait fish, such as capelin and candlefish. These so-called by-catch are routinely netted along with shrimp but are not typically counted, because they are not important to fish markets. They are, however, the meals for commercial fish and as such are as worthy of care as their flashier predators.

The by-catch turned out to be the big catch after all. What Anderson saw was that capelin fell off when shrimp did, whereas cod and pollack increased. At the same time, the crab fishery crashed, and salmon numbers rose (while prices, consequently, sank). "There was something that happened in the North Pacific that changed the whole ecological structure," Otto says.

"We may be right in the middle of a shift back; people just don't know," Duffy remarks. He speculates that salmon may be plentiful because it is simply a salmon period. "When the fishery was under the feds, it was downtime for salmon, and the government workers were criticized as idiots for not managing it well. Maybe the state is not good or bad. Maybe salmon are just doing what they do."

The changes in bait fish numbers could be the result of the growth of hatcheries. These outfits release young fish each spring to feed in the Sound and the Gulf of Alaska before they return home to spawn. These fish are, however, additions to the ecosystem—"extras" in a way—and they may be devouring bait fish that would have been available to wild fish and animals. Or the bait fish fluxes may be related to even bigger trends, such as those observed by Thomas C. Royer, an oceanographer at the University of Alaska-Fairbanks. Royer began taking water samples in 1970 and has concluded that the temperature fluctuates by two degrees Celsius every 15 to 25 years—shifts that could dramatically alter fish distribution.

In addition, he has gathered evidence that salinity shifts in 10- to 11-year cycles. Salinity differences could alter the way water flows through the Sound, changing the amount of nutrients available in the upper layers of the water column and disrupting the food chain. "I keep preaching that we need long-term studies," Royer comments, adding that many natural cycles are so long, however, that funders lose interest in them. "The funding for science is declining dramatically. There is just a great deal of frustration."

When there is suddenly a large influx of money into a poorly studied ecosystem—and finally the opportunity to do in-depth work—there is bound to be similar frustration. More money flooded into Prince William Sound after the *Exxon Valdez* spill than has flowed after any other. But, clearly, wherever litigation and science intersect, there is little hope for a frame with an expansive view. The federal rules governing damage assessment were recently modified to protect against another scientific fiasco after the next big spill; the new provisions try to ensure data sharing and to eliminate duplicative effort. Yet many observers doubt whether these changes will make any difference if billions of dollars are at stake. "I am not convinced at all that once we had the next big one everyone wouldn't go to their respective battle stations—'I have my science, and you have yours,'" comments David Kennedy of NOAA.

A Delicate Balance

Beyond the quality of science lies the public interpretation of science. Even though NOAA has shown that cleaning up can do more harm than good, demands to clean up persist. The Alaskan native village of Chenega has paid close attention to the spill-related research. Many of the residents of this community on Evans Island in the Sound are concerned about the oil's persistence.

Chenega residents thought the oil was having a biological effect, Piper says. "But there is nothing to show that it did. So are we going to spend a lot of money to clean up when there is no problem?" he asks. But science was not the point; ridding the beaches of unsightly oil was. "It was more an issue of trashing the neighborhood. It was a very legitimate complaint," Piper explains. And so the Trustees, who go through a public review process before they allocate their funds, will spend $1.9 million next summer to apply de-oiling compounds, at least one of which is known to be toxic to intertidal organisms.

Chenega is not alone. Ultimately, it is the frame of the television set and the mind-set of the media that dictate people's responses to images of oiled animals. The public wants the animals saved—at $80,000 per otter and $10,000 per eagle—even if the stress of their salvation kills them. "Scientists waste a lot of time saying, 'Do nothing,'" Duffy notes. "You have to balance the show and the science."

The Philippines and Indonesia are a case study in the aquarium fish trade. Ever wonder where all those brightly colored, tropical fish living in fish tanks come from? Many are captured alive from coral reefs in Southeast Asia and shipped to pet stores in the United States and around the world.

Practices used to catch coral-reef fish can be more harmful than most people realize. In the Philippines and Indonesia, reefs are sprayed with a poison called cyanide that slows the fish down long enough to be caught by swimmers with hand nets. This method is destructive to the ocean environment—the cyanide kills many of the reef fish and the reef itself. Large efforts are underway to stop cyanide fishing and better control the aquarium trade, with the long-term goal of saving coral reefs. If something isn't done soon, the reefs in the Philippines and Indonesia may not have any fish left to catch. —KW

"Fishy Business"
by Sarah Simpson
Scientific American, July 2001

Cyanide is one of the fastest-acting poisons known to science. Once ingested, it cripples the body's ability to transport oxygen and begins asphyxiating tissues almost instantly. At higher dosages it slows the heart and even stops electrical activity in the brain. Given cyanide's lethal nature, it is difficult to imagine that squirting the substance at coral-reef fish is a good way to catch them alive. And yet that's common practice in the Philippines and Indonesia, whose collectors supply some 85 percent of the tropical fish that enliven the world's saltwater aquariums.

Disabling agile fish with cyanide makes it easier for divers to capture them before they hide among branches or crevices in the coral, but the consequences are severe. Some experts estimate that half of the poisoned fish die on the reef, and 40 percent of those that survive the initial blast are dead before they reach an aquarium. This startling mortality rate doesn't encompass the devastation to the living corals, invertebrates and nontarget fish in the path of the toxic plume.

Cyanide fishing is only one of several human activities—including poor forestry practices and industrial pollution—that are destroying coral reefs worldwide. But to many marine biologists, cyanide is one of the biggest dangers in Southeast Asian waters. The region harbors nearly 30 percent of the planet's coral reefs and boasts the greatest diversity of marine life anywhere—at least for now. According to two regional surveys published last year, only 4.3 percent of Philippine reefs and only 6.7 percent of those in Indonesia are still in excellent condition. And it is those reefs that live-fish collectors typically target.

For nearly 20 years, efforts to reform destructive aspects of the aquarium trade have fallen primarily on the shoulders of the export countries, with limited success as a result. Now a new strategy is placing more opportunity for reef preservation in the hands of importers, retailers and consumers along the trade route. In an ambitious campaign that could help save some of Southeast Asia's last pristine reefs, an international nonprofit organization called the Marine Aquarium Council (MAC) is developing a method for guaranteeing that the marine fish sold in pet stores are collected in an ecofriendly manner. By this fall MAC officials expect to have the first "certified" fish for sale in the U.S.

"There has never been a system to define, identify and verify environmentally sound practices and products in this industry," says the council's executive director, Paul Holthus. "We are also labeling these products so that the consumers can reward those who are responsible."

Because only a handful of the prized fish species can be raised in captivity, the fate of the aquarium hobby lies in preserving the reefs. Aquarium owners know this, Holthus explains, and that is why he believes they will demand certified fish—if given the choice. Even today retailers have no way of knowing the exact origins of the fish they buy from importers. For most of the history of the aquarium trade, people's choices have been limited by scant scientific evidence and by conflicting anecdotes about the severity and exact locations of cyanide use and other destructive activities.

Tainted from the Start

Cyanide use in catching aquarium fish goes back
nearly to the origins of the industry in 1957, when a

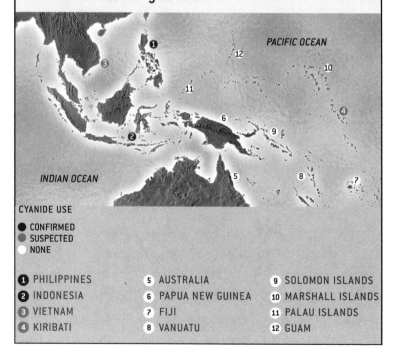

Exporters of Marine Aquarium Fish

About 85 percent of the world export of marine aquarium
species comes from the Philippines and Indonesia.
Together these two countries also make Southeast Asia
the world leader in cyanide use for the collection of live
fish. The practice originated with the Philippine aquarium
trade in the early 1960s and spread to northern
Indonesia in the early 1990s.

PACIFIC OCEAN

INDIAN OCEAN

CYANIDE USE
● CONFIRMED
● SUSPECTED
○ NONE

❶ PHILIPPINES	❺ AUSTRALIA	❾ SOLOMON ISLANDS
❷ INDONESIA	❻ PAPUA NEW GUINEA	❿ MARSHALL ISLANDS
❸ VIETNAM	❼ FIJI	⓫ PALAU ISLANDS
❹ KIRIBATI	❽ VANUATU	⓬ GUAM

Filipino entrepreneur shipped the first live fish to the U.S. in a tin can. Since the early 1960s, aquarium-fish collectors have squirted more than a million kilograms of cyanide onto Philippine reefs, according to estimates by the International Marinelife Alliance (IMA), a non-profit organization founded in 1985 to fight the spread of destructive fishing practices in the region. Over the past 15 years, the organization has spent $1 million to train fishermen to use hand nets instead of poison. But progress is slow, explains IMA co-founder Vaughan R. Pratt, who directs the organization's operations throughout Southeast Asia. Adequate training can take several months, and until collectors become skilled with hand nets, they can earn more money using cyanide.

When news of cyanide fishing broke in the U.S. in the late 1980s, the gossip among hobbyists was that cyanide was a harmless anesthetic if used in the proper doses, Pratt says. Mortality rates of collected fish were often high, but for the most part aquarium hobbyists chalked that up to the notoriously fragile nature of the fish. Any number of problems along the trade route— poor water quality or too much time enclosed in a plastic bag, for example—can kill fish in transit.

Meanwhile the marine aquarium hobby was flourishing in the U.S. and Europe. Innovations in aquarium technology and animal husbandry were improving people's ability to maintain diversified tanks. This success boosted demand not only for fish but also for corals, anemones and other live reef species. According to a 1999 report by the South Pacific

Forum Secretariat, an estimated 700,000 American households were keeping marine aquariums by 1992— a 60 percent rise in two years.

In the face of this increased demand for live fish— and because many Philippine reefs had been destroyed—cyanide fishing had spread to the northernmost island of Indonesia by the early 1990s. The most recent observations of IMA workers implicate nearby Vietnam and Kiribati as well [see box on page 178].

For decades, reef-conservation workers on the front lines in the Philippines did not have the cooperation of the import countries to back their efforts. That is exactly what the Marine Aquarium Council has to offer. This past spring a 60-member MAC committee made up of representatives from industry, conservation, government agencies and academia outlined standards for managing the fish and the reefs in a sustainable way. The idea is to forge a reliable chain of custody in which fish are handled appropriately at each step of the trade route, from reef to retailer. One team is spending the summer motivating a string of collectors and exporters in the Philippines to comply with MAC standards, and another group is soliciting support from importers and retailers in the U.S.

Forging an Unbroken Chain

A promising point of origin for a certifiable trade route is the city of Bagac, about 90 miles west of Manila. This community of some 21,000 residents lies nestled between the South China Sea and the checkerboard pattern of bright green rice paddies along the flanks of Mount Bataan.

Of the city's 2,500 fishermen, perhaps 30 are aquarium-fish collectors who live with their families in a beachfront cluster of thatch and wood buildings. This group of men (only men fish here) has been collecting fish without cyanide for the past seven years. Before that, cyanide fishing was all they knew. The turning point for them was meeting IMA's Philippines field director Ferdinand Cruz.

Cruz, who is also a member of MAC, knows the aquarium trade in the Philippines as well as anyone. He was drawn to the fishing communities shortly after he and his sister and mother opened an aquarium-fish export business in Manila in 1984. Almost immediately the family was perplexed by the high death rate of the fish. "We thought our facility was at fault at first," Cruz recalls. When he visited his collectors, they hid their cyanide because it was illegal. Those who admitted to using the poison reasoned that the practice was a harmless way to catch fish alive.

Cruz wasn't convinced. He went out in the boats with the cyanide users and saw dead fish floating in buckets, dead fish on the seafloor and fish convulsing after being squirted. "Six months later I noticed that reefs that had been sprayed were dying and full of algae," he says. "I kept going back to the areas where cyanide was used and made my own opinion that it was a very damaging chemical" [see "How Cyanide Kills," on the next page].

How Cyanide Kills

Although the intention of cyanide-wielding fish collectors is merely to stun their targets, the technique gives new meaning to the word "overkill." The most harrowing estimates suggest that half of the poisoned fish die on the reef, and many more die of health complications before they reach an aquarium.

Divers typically crush one or two white tablets of sodium cyanide into a plastic squeeze bottle. They then squirt the milky fluid—dissolved hydrogen cyanide and particles of the tablets—directly into the corals where the fish hide. The animals within reach of the plume ingest the cyanide ions through their mouths or the soft membranes of their gills. Once inside the fishes' bodies, the poison instantly begins disabling enzymes such as cytochrome oxidase, which accounts for significant oxygen uptake in living cells. The resulting asphyxiation stuns some fish and sends others into spasms, making them easy to grab by hand or net.

The poison tends to accumulate in the blood-rich liver, but studies conducted on freshwater fish also reveal acute damage to the spleen, heart and brain. Researchers point out that marine fish retain fluids in their bodies longer than their freshwater cousins do, giving cyanide more time to do harm before it is metabolized and excreted. Hydrogen cyanide concentrations of five milligrams per liter have proved lethal to certain fish—an exceedingly weak dosage considering that the

Nature Conservancy seized cyanide bottles in 1998 that contained concentrations greater than 1,500 milligrams per liter.

Most evidence of cyanide damage to corals is anecdotal, but a handful of scientific studies show that these animals don't fare much better than the fish. Marine biologist James M. Cervino, now a doctoral candidate at the University of South Carolina, witnessed destruction of corals in Southeast Asia when he was working with the Global Coral Reef Alliance, a nonprofit group based in Chappaqua, N.Y. During six years of fieldwork, Cervino grew tired of hearing people claim that cyanide does not kill corals, in response, he set out to garner laboratory evidence of the poison's ill effects.

In a series of experiments completed last year, Cervino exposed 10 species of coral to cyanide concentrations thousands of times lower than those that cyanide fishermen use. Eight of the coral species died immediately; the other two died within three months. The worst news was that the *Acropora* and other branching corals—the most important reef builders—were the most vulnerable. "If you're a little fish, you're going to hide among the branching corals," Cervino points out—which means that fish collectors will squirt those corals more often.

The cyanide disrupted the symbiotic relation between the coral host and its zooxanthellae. These algae give the coral animals their vibrant color, nourish them via

continued on following page

continued from previous page

photosynthesis and convert their waste into amino acids. Even the lowest cyanide dose (only 50 milligrams per liter) caused the zooxanthellae to erupt out of the corals in a glob of mucus, a process known as bleaching. And although the nonbranching corals proved more resistant to the poison, Cervino says, their outer tissues eventually began sloughing off like the skin of a burn victim.

Cruz worked for several years trying to keep his export warehouse cyanide-free, but he finally deemed that goal impossible to achieve. In 1993 he decided to abandon the business and began to work full-time for IMA. Since then, he has helped train some 2,500 of the estimated 4,000 aquarium-fish collectors in the Philippines. Cruz teaches them to set up barrier nets in canyons or deep fissures between coral heads and then herd the fish toward the net. Like most collectors in Southeast Asia, those in the Philippines breathe underwater through long, flexible plastic hoses called hookahs, which typically deliver air from an old compressor on board the fisherman's canoe. The diver holds the hookah in his teeth and often uses the bubbles from his exhalations to flush fish out of crevices in the coral and into the waiting nets.

Trained net fishermen are critical to a sustainable aquarium trade, but exporters also play a key role in MAC's plan. Most of the exporters, who constitute the next step in the chain of custody, are based in Manila. There, in warehouses filled with tanks, new arrivals typically mix with fish collected elsewhere around the country, many of them with cyanide. To make certification work, export warehouses will be required to quarantine fish that come from certified collectors.

At the warehouses, some fish can also be tested for cyanide exposure. Thanks in part to the efforts of Pratt and other IMA workers, cyanide detection laboratories are already in place. In 1991 the Philippines Bureau of Fisheries and Aquatic Resources contracted IMA to begin testing random samples of confiscated fish. The first detection laboratory opened near the Manila airport in 1991, and by early this year six laboratories around the country had tested more than 32,000 fish.

No current test can detect cyanide in living fish, so an unlucky few must be sacrificed. Chemists inspect and weigh each fish and liquefy it in a blender. The fish mush is distilled in a strong, hot acid so that any cyanide is liberated as hydrogen cyanide gas and then absorbed by a solution of sodium hydroxide. Electrode probes select for cyanide ions in the solution, enabling technicians to calculate cyanide levels in parts per million. Between 1996 and 1999, for example, workers saw the proportion of cyanide-tainted fish drop from 43 to 8 percent—a sign that IMA's investments are paying off.

Based on the considerable challenges of forging a certifiable chain of custody in the Philippines, Holthus says, the standards should be easy to maintain in

Hawaii, Australia and other regions that already have high-quality operations in place. Once a chain of custody is certifiable in the export countries, it's up to importers and retailers in the U.S. to choose to buy those certified fish—and to live up to the MAC guidelines for their own handling practices. Even with the cooperation of importers, turning the poison tide in Indonesia, where fewer collectors are properly trained, will not be as easy. "If certification fails or only half-succeeds in the Philippines," Cruz cautions, "MAC standards will not take off in Indonesia."

Peter J. Rubec, who co-founded IMA with Pratt and works as a fisheries biologist with the Florida Marine Research Institute in St. Petersburg, hopes that the efforts of IMA and MAC will "provide the scientific evidence needed to convince the industry that net-caught fish are a viable economic alternative to cyanide-caught fish." Some retailers aren't so sure. "The pressure in the marketplace today is for lower prices, not higher ones," says James A. Bennett, owner of an aquarium retail store in Portland, Ore. "If MAC's plan increases the cost of the fish, that's not going to work."

Holthus hopes that certification will not actually cost the consumer any more. If the system works, he says, then the money saved by reducing fish mortality could offset any increased costs of certification. The MAC standards require that no more than 1 percent of each species die at any given point in the chain of custody. Achieving this goal, Rubec believes, would be a tremendous feat. He estimates that at least 10 percent of cyanide-caught fish die at each step in the trade route.

What is more, the fish grow considerably in value from one end of the trade route to the other. An orange-and-white-striped clownfish bought from a Filipino collector for about 10 cents, for instance, will sell for $25 or more in an American pet store. With that kind of markup, Rubec and others argue that the industry should be able to absorb the remaining additional costs of certification.

Not Soon Enough for Some

Only time will tell whether economic obstacles will stymie MAC's mission. A few certified fish will be available to certain U.S. consumers this fall, but it may take a while for the desires of the market to force the aquarium trade to comply with the MAC standards. For some reef experts, the wait is agonizing.

"I don't think the Marine Aquarium Council has been tough enough," says marine biologist James M. Cervino, now a doctoral candidate at the University of South Carolina. After seeing cyanide damage for himself during his six years of service with the Global Coral Reef Alliance, Cervino argues that the trade should be halted temporarily: "If you don't have evidence that your fish were caught in a sustainable way, I can't see [this trade] being allowed to continue."

International law already bans the trade of thousands of species of stony coral under the Convention on the International Trade in Endangered Species of

Wild Fauna and Flora (CITES), but most of the coral-reef animals in the aquarium trade are not listed. Some local village governments in the Philippines have experimented with export bans on certain live reef species, but Cruz says that the restrictions just drove the fishermen to other illegal activities. He has been campaigning for local governments to grant fishing licenses as an alternative way to regulate collection. "If this trade does not prove to be sustainable, then it will have to close completely," Cruz warns. "In the meantime, we should still use the resources the right way so that the community can profit from it."

After a certification system is up and running, import restrictions in the U.S. could tighten the loop. Last fall the U.S. Coral Reef Task Force, established by an executive order in 1998, helped to draft legislation that would ensure that consumer demand for marine aquarium organisms does not contribute to the degradation of reefs and their inhabitants, as it does today, says task-force member Barbara A. Best. The trade recommendations, which were still being considered by Congress in mid-May, reflect MAC's philosophy that certification is a way to encourage responsible and sustainable trade. The legislation also provides that after an unspecified period of time, the U.S. should ban the import of any coral-reef species unless it is accompanied by official documentation that the animal was not collected through the use of destructive fishing practices.

"Industry-certification schemes can be quite slow in catching on, and legislation that required certification would speed up the process," explains Best, who also advises the U.S. Agency for International Development on marine resource and policy issues. "I have had some retailers tell me that they view the trade recommendations as one way to ensure that everyone carries animals that are being collected sustainably and treated humanely," Best says. "This would also ensure that those retailers that are behaving responsibly and carrying certified products are not undermined by lower prices from other retailers."

"I would adapt, because all of my competitors would have to do the same," says Bennett, who has seriously considered eliminating sales of live marine fish from his Portland aquarium store. "Some of us would invest a lot of money in a hurry and try to farm these things."

Even with legislative restrictions and a strong consumer demand for certified fish working in tandem, coral reefs in certain export countries may still be at risk. Indeed, the first MAC-certified fish may not actually be cyanide-free. A few tainted fish may slip through this initial testing phase of MAC's long-term plan, in which the standards are intentionally basic so that they can be met relatively quickly. "We'll raise the bar as we go along," Holthus says. During the next two years, MAC will design more detailed standards, and the organization will monitor the health of the reefs as the changes take place.

Even if MAC's certification works to curtail cyanide use among aquarium-fish collectors, some

Ways to Stop Cyanide Fishing

Anyone who wants to argue that cyanide fishing does not damage coral reefs should consider one important fact: the practice is forbidden in most of Southeast Asia. In 1975 a presidential decree in the Philippines made it illegal to fish with cyanide, possess it on a boat or sell fish caught with it, and Indonesia followed suit 10 years later. But cyanide still has several legitimate uses in industry—extracting gold from ore, for example—so the poison's importation is not strictly regulated. Clever criminals, along with government corruption and political strife, make enforcement extraordinarily difficult. That's why the International Marinelife Alliance, the Marine Aquarium Council and dozens of other organizations are pursuing a variety of strategies to halt this lethal—and illicit—practice.

1. Confiscate random samples of live fish from export warehouses and test them for cyanide exposure.
2. Train aquarium fishers to use proper collecting techniques: hand nets rather than poison or other chemicals.
3. Label fish that were caught without cyanide so that fish buyers can choose to support practices that preserve the reefs.
4. Encourage fishing communities to keep foreign fishers and illegal activities out of their local waters.

5. License aquarium collectors in export countries in order to limit their effects on the reefs.

6. Restrict the import of live coral-reef species that are not accompanied by documentation that they were captured without poison.

researchers worry that there is still no guarantee that fish collection will not degrade the reefs. A case in point is Kona, Hawaii. Although aquarium-fish collectors do not use cyanide in this area, Brian N. Tissot of Washington State University in Vancouver, Wash., and Leon E. Hallacher of the University of Hawaii at Hilo discovered in late 1999 that the collectors' activities were stunting the populations of seven species of coral-reef fishes, three of which are herbivores. Without these grazing fish to keep algae in check, the prolific plants could eventually suffocate the coral animals.

Another challenge is reducing destructive practices among collectors of live food fish, who have spread cyanide use into Malaysia, the Marshall Islands, Papua New Guinea and possibly other areas of Southeast Asia.

Cruz and other IMA officials have reported that these fishermen often make forays into coastal areas where they have little interest in the long-term productivity of the reefs. Aquarium-fish collectors, on the other hand, are mainly people from local communities that have been relying on the same reefs for their livelihoods for generations. In part on Cruz's recommendation, MAC's certification standards require that local fishermen protect their own turf, even if that means patrolling coastal waters and chasing outsiders away— a practice that Cruz has already helped implement in several Filipino villages.

Creating strong incentives for local fishermen to be responsible for managing their own reefs "is probably the best hope in most of these areas for ever conserving the reefs," Holthus says. He has also seen growing interest among certain players in the live food fish trade to set up their own certification scheme. Better still, reefs might be developed into tourist areas for divers or protected parks where no fishing is allowed. But because of economic and political barriers, only a small number of reefs will ever fall into these categories.

The bottom line according to Cruz: If cyanide fishing isn't stopped, a lot of these reefs will be gone in a few decades. The good news, he believes, is that the battle against cyanide use in the Philippines is no longer uphill.

Sarah Simpson is a staff editor and writer. Additional reporting by Gary Braasch.

Web Sites

Due to the changing nature of Internet links, the Rosen Publishing Group, Inc., has developed an online list of Web sites related to the subject of this book. This site is updated regularly. Please use this link to access the list:

http://www.rosenlinks.com/saca/ocea

For Further Reading

Ballard, Robert. *Adventures in Ocean Exploration: From the Discovery of the Titanic to the Search for Noah's Flood*. Washington, DC: National Geographic, 2001.

Bigg, Grant R. *The Oceans and Climate*. Cambridge, England: Cambridge University Press, 2003.

Byatt, Andrew, Alastair Fothergill, Martha Holmes, and British Broadcasting Corporation. *Blue Planet*. New York, NY: DK Publishing, 2002.

Carson, Rachel. *The Sea Around Us*. New York, NY: Oxford University Press, 1951.

Goldstein, Natalie. *How Do We Know the Nature of the Ocean?* New York, NY: Rosen Publishing Group, 2005.

Greenlaw, Linda. *The Hungry Ocean: A Swordboat Captain's Journey*. New York, NY: Hyperion, 1999.

McGonigal, David. *Antarctica: The Blue Continent*. New York, NY: Firefly Books, 2003.

McPhee, John. *The Founding Fish*. New York, NY: Farrar, Straus, and Giroux, 2002.

National Research Council. *Marine Mammals and Low Frequency Sound*. Washington, DC: National Academy Press, 2000.

Rozwadowski, Helen. *Fathoming the Ocean: The Discovery and Exploration of the Deep Sea*. Cambridge, MA: Harvard University Press, 2005.

Safina, Carl. *Song for a Blue Ocean*. New York, NY: Henry Holt and Company, 1997.

Bibliography

Anderson, Donald M. "Red Tides." *Scientific American*, Vol. 271, No. 2, August 1994, pp. 62–68.

Boyd, Claude E., and Jason W. Clay. "Shrimp Aquaculture and the Environment." *Scientific American*, Vol. 278, No. 6, June 1998, pp. 58–65.

Falkowski, Paul G. "The Ocean's Invisible Forest." *Scientific American*, Vol. 287, No. 2, August 2002, pp. 54–61.

Holloway, Marguerite. "Diversity Blues." *Scientific American*, Vol. 271, No. 2, August 1994, pp. 16–18.

Holloway, Marguerite. "Sounding Out Science." *Scientific American*, Vol. 275, No.1, October 1996, pp. 106–112.

Kasting, James F. "The Origins of Water on Earth." *Scientific American Special Edition: New Light on the Solar System*, Vol. 13, No. 3, 2003, pp. 28–33.

Nybakken, James W., and Steven K. Webster. "Life in the Ocean." *Scientific American Presents: The Oceans*, Vol. 9, No. 3, 1998, pp. 74–86.

Pauly, Daniel, and Reg Watson. "Counting the Last Fish." *Scientific American*, Vol. 289, No. 1, July 2003, pp. 42–47.

Schneider, David. "Alarming Nets." *Scientific American*, Vol. 275, No. 3, September 1996, pp. 40–42.

Schneider, David. "Down and Out in the Gulf of Mexico." *Scientific American*, Vol. 272, No. 4, April 1995, p. 29.

Schneider, David. "The Rising Seas." *Scientific American*, Vol. 276, No. 3, March 1997, pp. 112–117.

Simpson, Sarah. "Fishy Business." *Scientific American*, Vol. 285, No. 1, July 2001, pp. 83–89.

Simpson, Sarah. "Melting Away." *Scientific American*, Vol. 282, No. 1, January 2000, pp. 19–20.

Yam, Philip. "The Man Who Would Hear Ocean Temperatures." *Scientific American*, Vol. 272, No. 1, January 1995, pp. 38–40.

Index

About the Editor

Krista West has long loved the oceans. She studied marine biology at the University of Washington in Seattle, where she took up scuba diving and learned much about life in the sea. She also has a masters of science in earth and environmental journalism from Columbia University and has been published extensively in the field. Today she lives with her family in Fairbanks, Alaska.

Illustration Credits

Cover: Andrew J. Martinez/Photo Researchers, Inc.; p. 14 David Schneider; p. 18 Edward Bell; p. 28 William F. Haxby and Dmitry Krasny; p. 47 Cleo Vilett; p. 56 Nina Finkel (graph) and Cleo Vilett; p. 68 Roberto Osti; p. 70 Jennifer Christiansen (Source: U.N. Food and Agriculture Organization); pp. 110, 112 William F. Haxby; p. 143 David Fierstein; p. 178 Laurie Grace (Sources: Marine Aquarium Council, International Marinelife Alliance).

Series Designer: Tahara Anderson
Series Editor: Brian Belval